Christmas
▲ ▲ ▲ COUNTRY-STYLE ▲ ▲ ▲

Welcome to the uplifting sights, scents, sounds and spirit of Christmas...in the country!

A Christmas celebrated in the countryside is wonderfully different than one anywhere else, and this book presents you with all the makings for a memorable country-style family holiday. You'll find recipes for hearty, home-cooked meals and festive desserts...charming crafts that can be made in a jiffy for gifts or display

Doris Gehrig Barker

...true stories of blessings and inspiration from down-to-earth country-loving folks ...traditional Christmas carols to sing...as well as an original, read-aloud child's Nativity story with a touching country slant.

As yuletide spirits begin to soar once more in anticipation of the holidays, turn the pages of *Christmas Country-Style*

and turn your hearts toward the beauty and bounty of the season.

And keep in mind that this is just the first in a colorful series of *Christmas Country-Style* books we're planning to put together once a year. You can look forward to many more country Christmases to remember in the future!

Publisher: Roy Reiman
Editor: Linda Piepenbrink
Crafts Editor: Marjon Galvin
Editorial Assistant: Kristine Krueger
Art Director: Doris Schaffer
Art Assistants: Sue Myers, Charlotte Allmann
Production: Sally Manich, Ellen Lloyd
Food and craft photography by Mike
Huibregtse; p.3—Gene Ahrens; this page—
Robert Cushman Hayes; p.52—Richard
Abarno/The Stock Market; p.97—DPI.

© 1991 by Reiman Publications, L.P.
5400 S. 60th St., Greendale WI 53129

Printed in U.S.A.
International Standard Book Number: 0-89821-096-8
Library of Congress Catalog Card Number: 91-62465

♣ ♣ ♣ CONTENTS ♣ ♣ ♣

BAA-BAA

(Have you any wool?)

By Linda Piepenbrink

All night long it snowed and snowed
Until Doodle the Rooster crowed.
"Wake up! Wake up! It's already light.
We're having a birthday party tonight!"

"A birthday party?
For WHO? For WHO?"
The Old Owl asked,
without a clue.

"The party is
for a royal child,
Born in a stable,
meek and mild."

"In *our* stable?" asked Holly Horse.
"Yes," said Doodle, "right here, of course!
The baby needs a warm place to stay.
Will someone please help gather hay?"

"I will," said Gabby Goat with a grin
As she pulled fresh hay from a bin.
Then Holly Horse put a tree in the barn,
And strung it with apples and berries and yarn.

Miss Spider spun a cloth of silk
And Gernie Cow filled bottles with milk.
Kit-Cat took yarn and started to knit,
"I hope this baby cap will fit."

Duck-Duck pulled a feather from his wing,
"I'll make a pillow for the small king!"
Harriet Hen laid eggs for a cake,
"We must have cake for goodness sake!"

Grandma Goose honked the birthday song
And a flock of birdies sang along.
Patrick Pig—he went hog-wild—
He danced a jig for the coming child.

Then all at once came a thundering sound,
The animals jumped with fear from the ground.
"Baa-Baa Humbug!" bellowed Woolly the Sheep,
"Quit that racket, I'm trying to sleep!"

Illustrations by Lisa Horstman

HUMBUG!

Then Darla Dog barked, "Shame on you Woolly,
You frightened us, don't be such a bully!
Isn't there something a sheep can do?"
Darla added. "We're counting on you."

But Woolly the Sheep just huffed and said,
"Count me out, I'm staying in bed!"
Then Doodle saw the moon start to rise
And a star began to shine in his eyes.

"Get ready to sing," crowed Doodle, "they're coming."
Then all but Woolly could be heard humming…
"Away in a manger, no crib for a bed
The little Lord Jesus laid down His sweet head…"

Mary and Joseph soon hurried inside,
Mary was tired from her long journey's ride.
Then the animals lined up one by one
To see Mary's baby, her firstborn son.

She wrapped Him inside the cloth of silk
And nibbled on cake and fed Him milk.
She placed the cap on Jesus' head
And laid Him in the hay-filled bed.

Mary lay on the pillow to sleep
And the animals fell asleep in a heap.
Then Jesus began to softly cry
And Woolly the Sheep opened one eye.

The others didn't hear Him at all
So Woolly went to the baby so small.
He looked at the Child and then he knew
Exactly what a sheep can do.

With his warm wool, he cuddled the Child
And little baby Jesus looked up and smiled.

9

Silent Night

Joseph Mohr

Franz Gruber

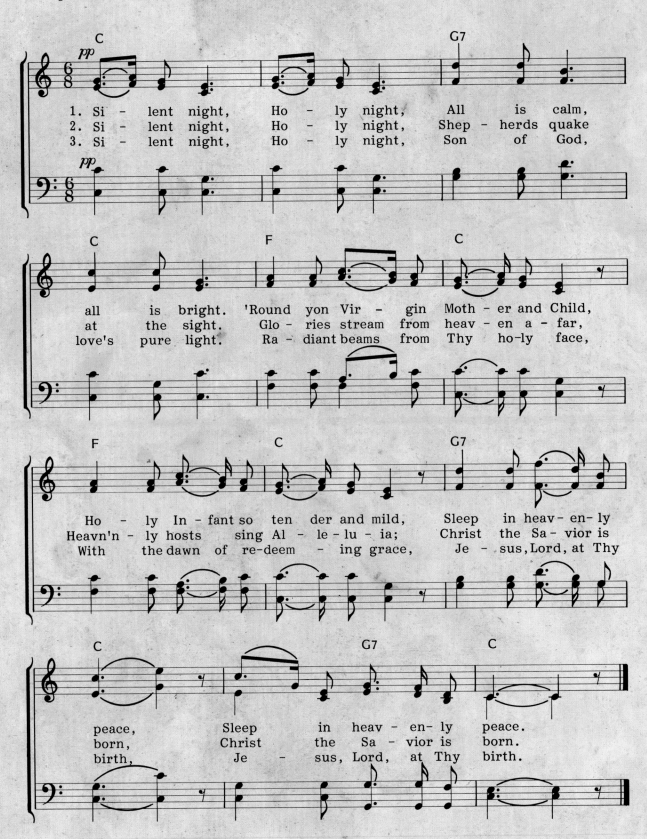

1. Si - lent night, Ho - ly night, All is calm, all is bright. 'Round yon Vir - gin Moth - er and Child, Ho - ly In - fant so ten - der and mild, Sleep in heav - en - ly peace, Sleep in heav - en - ly peace.

2. Si - lent night, Ho - ly night, Shep - herds quake at the sight. Glo - ries stream from heav - en a - far, Heavn'n - ly hosts sing Al - le - lu - ia; Christ the Sa - vior is born, Christ the Sa - vior is born.

3. Si - lent night, Ho - ly night, Son of God, love's pure light. Ra - diant beams from Thy ho - ly face, With the dawn of re - deem - ing grace, Je - sus, Lord, at Thy birth, Je - sus, Lord, at Thy birth.

Barn Holds True Christmas Spirit

AROUND Burlington, Wisconsin, farm wife Beverly Squire well may have the most curious Christmas list of all. When the holiday season nears, she sets out in search of *six sets* of parents and infants.

That's because, each December 24, the real story of Christmas unfolds right in her nephew's barn.

"'Christmas in the Barn' started simply as a gift to the community from our church and from our family," Beverly explains. "Back about 1969, my brother-in-law Everett (who lives next door) decided to concentrate on crops, and turned his dairy barn into a harvest produce center.

"At the same time, the pastor of our church—the English Settlement United Methodist Church—brought up the idea of staging an authentic Christmas service. Since the manger was sound, and the stalls had been freshly cleaned, Everett volunteered his barn. We've been celebrating Christmas Eve there ever since. My nephew John lives next door now and has

AWAY IN A MANGER, families gather for authentic Christmas Eve Nativity—portrayed on a family farm. That's Beverly Squire (at top), nephew John, his wife, Cindy, and their son, Andrew.

continued the tradition."

And doing so with a good supply of company! Six half-hour services on the day before Christmas re-create the Nativity—complete with lantern-lit manger, Bible readings, carols and straw bales for seating.

"We're expecting close to 1,000 people, from as far away as Michigan," Beverly notes. "For many

"Christmas Eve services in the barn have become a tradition!"

families, services on our farm have become a Christmas tradition."

Meanwhile, scouring the surrounding area for Christmas Eve "actors" has become standard fare for her. Children from the congregation temporarily turn into angels, shepherds and wise men. The Holy Family, portrayed by six different local couples and their babies, switches with each new service.

"They all consider it an honor," Beverly declares happily. "And now we've started on our *second* generation. The baby in one of last year's programs is the

daughter of our original Christmas angel 20 years ago!"

Neighboring farmers still active with animals also play an important part. "They donate their baby calves and sheep to us," Beverly details.

"Of course, we have a donkey, too—the same one's served us for 15 years now. Christmas Eve is the only day all year that donkey is bridled…and he always heads straight for the manger."

No one needs encouragement to visit the goody-filled hospitality table between services. "Our ladies bring in enough home baking to feed hundreds," Beverly reports. "The men have their own role—directing traffic…arranging bales… and fitting everyone in our barn!"

The quarters—just as on the very first Christmas Eve—*may* become close, Beverly admits. But the Squires have never turned anyone away. And, vows Beverly, they never will.

"There'll always be room in the 'inn'," she assures…especially on Christmas Eve.

The Squires mount a star atop their silo to guide visitors east from Burlington on Hwy. 11 to County Trunk J, north 2 miles on J to Church Road, then east 1 mile to 26715 Church Rd.

How Do You Spell 'Christmas'?

By Bernice Maddux
Weatherford, Texas

SURELY the ties of home are more binding at Christmas than at any other time of year.

Though we often try to tell ourselves we have outgrown all that, sweet and precious memories of past Christmases at home keep flooding our consciousness.

Suddenly we find ourselves longing for one more Christmas at home, just like the ones that still live in our hearts.

How do you spell "Christmas"? Most of us spell it "H-O-M-E". It may be that the home we shared for our early Christmases no longer exists, and that's sad. But subsequent homes do. Homes that have protected, sustained and beckoned us with open arms. No doubt the welcome mat is out there, and it's time to be on our way. It's Christmas!

Home may not be a fine mansion with grounds all spacious and fair. It may be old and drab and sadly in need of repair. Does that matter? Not in the least. We all know, and are acutely aware of it at Christmas, that home can be by the side of the road if the ones we love are there.

Whatever its location or condition, home has a certain feel of belonging, and we seek that comfort, especially at Christmas. It's a hang-up-your-coat, take-off-your-shoes, let-Christmas-begin sort of place. It's a friendly and caring place to let go of what's bothering us and refuel our starving souls.

As we share laughter, hopes and plans with those of a kindred spirit, our own troubles seem to melt along with the snow and ice on the warm roof above the Christmas fire.

What better place than home to sing the familiar carols that have endured the passing of years and the tests of time?

Christmas is a time for forgiving shortcomings, forgetting differences, and clasping hands and giving thanks to God for the beauties and bounties of home, as well as for its lasting hold on us.

And it's a time for worshipping, with dear ones in quiet places, the Christ Child of our yesterday, our today and our forever who gave us Christmas.

I'll see you at home on Christmas.

Christmas POETRY CORNER

HOLIDAY BLESSINGS

Lights twinkling
Sounds tinkling
Bells ringing
Folks singing
Snow falling
Friends calling
Gifts growing

Smiles glowing
Heads bowing
Hearts vowing
God's stressing
His blessing.

**Faye Tanner Cool
Anselmo, Nebraska**

Barbara Kirk/The Stock Market

Fred Sieb/H. Armstrong Roberts

Bob Taylor

COUNTRY CHRISTMAS

It's Christmas in the country,
The mantel's trimmed with cards;
Friends and neighbors far and near
Stop in with their regards.

A cheery wreath adorns the door,
An angel tops the tree,
And colored lights are strung about,
Twinkling merrily.

Mistletoe hangs from the door,
The children just can't wait;
Time seems to pass so slowly,
They want to celebrate.

Then when at last the day arrives,
There's magic in the air—
It's Christmas in the country,
And what a grand affair!

**Kathy A. Schaeffer
Sunbury, Pennsylvania**

CIRCLES OF THE SEASON

Gifts for friends and family
Circle round our Christmas tree;
And on each door new wreaths are seen—
Circles made of evergreen.

On winter nights with friends we share
A round of carols and a prayer;
As holding hands we make a ring,
And filled with joy we loudly sing.

Circles are the season's cheer—
It's Christmas rounding out the year!

Ericka Northrop, Tucson, Arizona

CANDLELIGHT FEAST

LIGHT THE CANDLES, turn up the carols and put the finishing touches on your Christmas Eve buffet. After weeks of anticipation and hours of preparation, it's finally time to enjoy the warmth and love of a country Christmas.

Gather family and friends around a sparkling table filled with these holiday favorites. Sample such distinctive ethnic dishes as cheese or potato-stuffed pierogi, tomato- and cheese-drenched mostaccioli, and spiced and sauced Swedish meatballs...filled with the traditional flavors that link generations. Expand your holiday horizons with regional favorites such as Swiss 'n' Crab Supper Pie, Oyster Cheese Appetizer Log, Christmas Vegetable Salad and a refreshing Cranberry Punch.

In a candlelit setting enhanced by family customs, give thanks for each other and for fine, festive food.

Clockwise from lower left: **Oyster Cheese Appetizer Log**, from Mrs. William Tracy, Jerseyville, Illinois; **Christmas Vegetable Salad**, from Mary Dean, Eau Claire, Wisconsin; **Celery En Casserole**, from Mary Lou Sipherd, Bishop, California; **Cranberry Punch**, from Deanna House, Portage, Michigan; **Swedish Meatballs**, from Emily Gould, Hawarden, Iowa; **Mostaccioli**, from Nancy Mundhenke, Kinsley, Kansas; **Polish Pierogi**, from Adeline Piscitelli, Sayreville, New Jersey; **Swiss 'n' Crab Supper Pie**, from Kathy Crow, Cordova, Alaska.

These recipes can be found on pages 17-18.

☃ SUGARPLUMS ☃

HELP YOURSELF to desserts rich with nostal-
gic tastes of Christmases past. Try lacy Scandinavian krumkake that crumbles delightfully on
the tongue, or delicate shortbread with a crisp,
buttery bite. For a sweet treat, there's a Christmas
citrus compote appropriately named Orange Appeal, and White Christmas Candy with red and
green peppermint crunch that looks and tastes like
Christmas. Enjoy…and happy holidays!

Clockwise from lower left: **Orange Appeal**, Billie
Moss, El Sobrante, California; **Shortbread**, Mrs. Allen
Swenson, Camdenton, Missouri; **Whipped Cream
Krumkake**, Imelda Nesteby, Decorah, Iowa; **White
Christmas Candy**, Carol Hammond, Helena, Alabama.

These recipes can be found on page 18.

Apple Candles Add Natural Glow

ADD "A-PEEL" to your holiday table settings with candles like those shown in the photo at left, crafted from real apples!

You'll need large, bright-red apples with flat bases, plus white votive candles and paraffin wax.

Polish the apples by rubbing briskly with a soft cloth. Trace the outline of a candle on top of each apple with permanent marker and, using a sharp paring knife, carefully cut around the marked outline.

With a melon baller, remove the marked section of each apple deep enough to hold the candle. (Place hollowed apples in a solution of diluted citrus juice to prevent browning while completing all candles.)

Carefully melt paraffin wax (one block for every six candles) in a heavy saucepan. Dry the apples with a paper towel; insert votive candles and slowly pour melted paraffin around candles to fill empty space (about 2 tablespoons per candle). Let them stand to firm up.

You may burn these candles more than once—they'll keep several days.

OYSTER CHEESE APPETIZER LOG

Mrs. William Tracy, Jerseyville, Illinois

- 3 packages (8 ounces *each*) cream cheese, softened
- 2 tablespoons bottled steak sauce
- 1/4 cup creamy salad dressing
- 1 garlic clove, minced *or* 1 teaspoon garlic powder
- 1 small onion, finely chopped
- 2 cans (3-3/4 ounces *each*) smoked oysters, well drained and chopped
- 3 cups chopped pecans, *divided*
- 3 tablespoons chili powder

Chopped fresh parsley

In mixer bowl, blend together cheese, steak sauce, salad dressing, garlic and onion. Stir in the oysters and 1 cup pecans. Shape into long cylinder (a French loaf baking pan works well). Roll in mixture of chili powder, remaining pecans and parsley. **Yield:** 18-inch log (2-1/2-inch diameter).

POLISH PIEROGI

Adeline Piscitelli, Sayreville, New Jersey

DOUGH:
- 4 cups all-purpose flour
- 2 eggs
- 1/2 cup sour cream
- 1 teaspoon salt
- 2/3 cup warm water

POTATO FILLING:
- 3 medium potatoes (about 1 pound), cooked, drained and mashed
- 1/2 medium onion, chopped
- 1/4 cup butter

Salt and pepper to taste

CHEESE FILLING:
- 1 pound dry cottage cheese
- 2 eggs, beaten
- 1/2 teaspoon salt
- 1/4 cup butter, melted

SAUCE:
- 1 large onion, chopped
- 1/2 cup butter

To make dough, combine all ingredients, adding water a little at a time. Knead dough until firm and elastic; cover with a bowl and let rest 10 minutes. For potato and cheese fillings, combine all ingredients and mix. Divide dough into three parts. On floured surface, roll dough to 1/8-in. thick; cut into 3-in. rounds with cutter. Place a small spoonful of filling in center of each round; fold and press edges together firmly to seal. Drop pierogi in simmering chicken bouillon with 1 teaspoon oil. Do not crowd. Simmer for 15 minutes, stirring gently with wooden spoon to prevent sticking. Remove with slotted spoon; drain well. Saute onion and butter until golden. Placed drained pierogi in casserole and pour sauce over all. **Yield:** 7 dozen.

SWEDISH MEATBALLS

Emily Gould, Hawarden, Iowa

- 1-2/3 cups evaporated milk, *divided*
- 2/3 cup chopped onion
- 1/4 cup fine dry bread crumbs
- 1/2 teaspoon salt
- 1/2 teaspoon allspice

Dash pepper
- 1 pound ground round
- 2 teaspoons butter
- 2 beef bouillon cubes
- 1 cup boiling water
- 1/2 cup cold water
- 2 tablespoons all-purpose flour
- 1 tablespoon lemon juice

Combine 2/3 cup evaporated milk, onion, crumbs and seasonings. Add the meat; mix well, chill. Shape meat mixture into 1-in. balls. In a large skillet, brown meatballs in butter. Dissolve bouillon cubes in boiling water; pour over meatballs and bring to boil over medium heat. Cover and simmer for 15 minutes. Meanwhile, blend together cold water and flour. Remove meatballs from skillet, skim fat from pan juices and reserve juices. Stir remaining evaporated milk and flour/water mixture into pan juices in skillet; cook, uncovered, over low heat, stirring until sauce thickens. Return meatballs to skillet. Stir in lemon juice. Serve with cooked noodles, tossed with poppy seeds and butter, if desired. **Yield:** 3-1/2 dozen 1-inch meatballs.

CHRISTMAS VEGETABLE SALAD

Mary Dean, Eau Claire, Wisconsin

- 2 cups thinly sliced cauliflower
- 1/2 cup sliced stuffed green olives
- 1/3 cup chopped green pepper
- 1/3 cup chopped red pepper

DRESSING:
- 1-1/2 tablespoons fresh lemon juice
- 1-1/2 tablespoons white wine vinegar
- 4 tablespoons vegetable oil
- 1 teaspoon salt
- 1/2 teaspoon sugar

Freshly ground black pepper

Combine cauliflower, olives and peppers in a glass bowl. Put all dressing ingredients in a jar; shake well and pour over vegetables. Marinate in refrigerator for several hours or overnight. **Yield:** 6-8 servings.

CELERY EN CASSEROLE

Mary Lou Sipherd, Bishop, California

- 4-1/2 cups diagonally sliced celery
- 1 can (5 ounces) sliced water chestnuts, drained
- 1/4 cup diced pimiento
- 1/4 cup slivered almonds
- 1 can (10-3/4 ounces) cream of chicken soup

TOPPING:
- 1/2 cup dry bread crumbs
- 4 teaspoons butter, melted
- 2 tablespoons sesame seeds
- 2 tablespoons grated Parmesan cheese

Cook the celery in water for 5 minutes or until crisp-tender. Drain; add the water chestnuts, pimiento, almonds and soup. Pour into 1-1/2-qt. buttered baking dish. Combine topping ingredients; sprinkle over top of casserole. Bake at 350° for 25 minutes or until crumbs are golden brown. **Yield:** 8 servings.

CRANBERRY PUNCH

Deanna House, Portage, Michigan

4 cups fresh *or* frozen
  cranberries
3-1/2 quarts water
12 whole cloves
4 sticks cinnamon (3 inches *each*)
3/4 cup orange juice
2/3 cup fresh lemon juice
2 cups sugar

In a Dutch oven or large kettle, combine cranberries, water, cloves and cinnamon. Bring to a boil; cover, reduce heat and simmer for 12-15 minutes. Strain the cooked juice through a fine sieve or cheesecloth, squeezing gently. To strained juice, add orange juice, lemon juice and sugar; stir until sugar dissolves. Serve piping hot. **Yield:** 25 1/2-cup servings.

MOSTACCIOLI

Nancy Mundhenke, Kinsley, Kansas

1-1/2 pounds bulk Italian sausage
4 cups meatless spaghetti sauce
1 pound mostaccioli, cooked
  and drained
1 egg, beaten
15 ounces ricotta cheese
2 cups (8 ounces) shredded
  mozzarella cheese
1/2 cup freshly grated Romano
  cheese
Fresh basil

In a Dutch oven, brown sausage; drain. Stir in spaghetti sauce and mostaccioli; set aside. In a bowl, combine egg, ricotta and mozzarella. In a 13-in. x 9-in. x 2-in. baking pan or 2-1/2- to 3-qt. casserole, spread half of the sausage mixture then all of the cheese mixture, and top with remaining sausage mixture. Bake, covered, at 375° for 40 minutes. Top with Romano cheese; bake 5 minutes more or until heated through. Garnish with fresh basil. **Yield:** 10-12 servings.

SWISS 'N' CRAB SUPPER PIE

Kathy Crow, Cordova, Alaska

1 unbaked pie crust (9 inches) *or*
  pastry-lined 9-1/2-inch tart pan
  with removable bottom
1 can (7-1/2 ounces) crab,
  drained, flaked and cartilage
  removed
1 cup (4 ounces) shredded
  Swiss cheese
2 green onions, sliced thin

3 eggs, beaten
1 cup light cream *or* evaporated
  milk
1/2 teaspoon salt
1/2 teaspoon grated lemon peel
1/4 teaspoon dry mustard
Dash mace
1/4 cup sliced unblanched
  almonds

Line unpricked pastry shell with heavy foil; fill with dry beans. Bake pastry at 450° for 5 minutes; take from oven, remove beans and foil. Arrange the crab evenly over crust. Top with cheese and onions. Combine remaining ingredients except almonds; pour into shell. Top with almonds. Bake at 325° for 45 minutes or until set. Remove from oven; let stand 10 minutes before serving. **Yield:** 10 servings.

SHORTBREAD

Mrs. Allen Swenson, Camdenton, Missouri

1/2 pound sweet butter, softened
  (*do not* substitute margarine)
1/2 teaspoon salt
1/2 cup sugar
1/2 cup sifted confectioners' sugar
2 cups all-purpose flour
1/2 cup cornstarch

In a mixing bowl, cream butter, salt and sugars. Sift together flour and cornstarch; gradually blend into creamed mixture. Shape dough into a 15-in. x 2-in. x 1-in. rectangle; chill. Slice rectangle into 1/4-in. thick cookies; place on ungreased cookie sheets. Make two fork prints on each cookie. Bake at 325° for 15-18 minutes. Don't overbake —*cookies will not brown*. Cool on wire rack. **Yield:** 5 dozen.

WHIPPED CREAM KRUMKAKE

Imelda Nesteby, Decorah, Iowa

3 large eggs
1 cup sugar
1/2 cup sweet butter, melted
1/2 cup whipping cream, whipped
1/2 teaspoon nutmeg
1-1/2 cups all-purpose flour
Sweet butter for krumkake plates
Whipped cream, optional

Beat eggs in mixing bowl until very light. Add sugar gradually, beating to blend. Slowly add butter, then cream and nutmeg. Mix in flour (dough will be consistency of cookie dough). Chill thoroughly. Preheat krumkake plates over medium heat for about 10 minutes or until a drop of water "dances" when

dropped on plates. Brush plates with sweet butter; place 1 slightly rounded tablespoon of dough in center of lower plate; close iron and press handles together. If excess dough comes outsides, remove with table knife. Bake for about 30 seconds; flip iron and bake for about 30 seconds on other side. Remove krumkake and immediately roll over cone-shaped form. Place, seam side down, on parchment paper to cool; remove form. Fill cooled cones with sweetened whipped cream, if desired. Serve immediately. **Yield:** about 3 dozen.

ORANGE APPEAL

Billie Moss, El Sobrante, California

8 to 10 large oranges
  (any variety)
4 tablespoons orange juice
  concentrate *or*
  orange-flavored liqueur
1/2 cup shredded coconut
1/2 cup blanched almonds,
  sliced
1/2 cup confectioners' sugar

Peel oranges, removing as much white membrane as possible. Cut in crosswise slices 1/4-in. thick *or* section as pictured. Arrange half of the orange slices or sections overlapping on a large platter or in the bottom of a round glass bowl. Sprinkle with concentrate or liqueur, coconut, almonds and half of the confectioners' sugar. Top with remaining oranges. Sprinkle with remaining sugar. Chill until serving time. Serve chilled on glass plates with tea cookies and coffee, if desired. **Yield:** 8 servings.

WHITE CHRISTMAS CANDY

Carol Hammond, Helena, Alabama

2 pounds white chocolate*
1/2 pound red and green
  peppermint stick crunch** *or*
  crushed candy canes *or*
  crushed peppermint candies

Melt chocolate over medium-low heat, stirring until smooth. Remove from heat; stir in crunch. Spread on parchment paper-lined cookie sheets; chill in refrigerator for 8-10 minutes. Break into small pieces; store in airtight containers. **Yield:** 2-1/2 pounds. (*White chocolate is available in candy and cake making specialty stores. **Peppermint stick crunch is available in 1-pound packages through Country Kitchen, Fort Wayne IN 46808. Call 1-219/482-4835 to order by phone.)

QUICK & EASY FESTIVE FOODS

WHEN FRIENDS are dropping in for the holidays and you don't have a lot of time to fuss in the kitchen, don't despair. Instead, try this quick-and-easy festive fare!

>>>>>>>>※<<<<<<<<<
SALMON/CUCUMBER APPETIZERS

Kay Schumacker, Batesville, Indiana

2 packages (3 ounces *each*) cream cheese
1/2 teaspoon salt
1/2 teaspoon dill weed
2 medium cucumbers, cut into 1/8-inch slices
1 can (16 ounces) red salmon, drained and bones removed
Pimiento

Combine cream cheese, salt and dill; mix until blended. Using a pastry bag with large star tip, pipe a star of cream cheese mixture onto each cucumber slice. Top each star with a small piece of salmon; garnish with a tiny piece of pimiento. Cover; refrigerate until ready to serve. **Yield:** about 2 dozen.

>>>>>>>>※<<<<<<<<<
EASY CHICKEN DIVAN CASSEROLE

Judy Merchant, Port Washington, Wisconsin

2 packages (10 ounces *each*) frozen broccoli, cut up, cooked and drained
2 cups cooked cubed chicken
2 cans (10-3/4 ounces *each*) cream of chicken soup, undiluted
1 cup mayonnaise
1 teaspoon to 1 tablespoon fresh lemon juice
1/2 teaspoon curry powder
TOPPING:
1/2 cup shredded cheddar cheese
1/2 cup soft bread crumbs
1 tablespoon butter

Combine broccoli and chicken in the bottom of a greased 13-in. x 9-in. x 2-in. baking pan. Set aside. In a bowl, combine soup, mayonnaise, lemon juice and curry powder; pour over chicken and broccoli. Combine topping ingredients; sprinkle over sauce. Bake at 350° for 30 minutes. **Yield:** 12 servings.

>>>>>>>>※<<<<<<<<<
DESSERT DIP FOR FRUIT

Joyce Fortney, Artemus, Kentucky

1 package (8 ounces) cream cheese, softened
2 tablespoons frozen orange juice concentrate
1 jar (7 ounces) marshmallow creme
Fresh fruit (orange sections, pineapple chunks, kiwi slices, apple wedges and banana chunks dipped in orange or lemon juice to prevent discoloration)

In a mixing bowl, combine cream cheese with the orange juice concentrate until smooth. Fold in marshmallow creme. Serve dip in a bowl in the center of a large glass plate, surrounded by assorted fruit.

>>>>>>>>※<<<<<<<<<
CRAB DELIGHTS

Marie Schomas, Homewood, Illinois

9 slices white bread
1 can (7-1/2 ounces) crabmeat, flaked
1 small onion, grated
1 cup (4 ounces) shredded cheddar cheese
1 cup mayonnaise
1 teaspoon curry powder
1/2 teaspoon salt

Remove crusts from bread; cut each slice into four squares, strips or triangles. Mix remaining ingredients; spread on bread. Place on baking sheet; broil until golden and bubbly. **Yield:** 36 appetizers.

>>>>>>>>※<<<<<<<<<
MEAT AND CHEESE COCKTAIL ROUNDS

Lisa Seaba, Muscatine, Iowa

1 pound lean ground beef
1 pound Italian sausage
1 pound American cheese, cubed
Garlic powder to taste
1 package party rye bread
Leaf oregano, crumbled

In a large skillet, brown meats. Drain fat. Add cheese and garlic powder; simmer until the cheese melts, stirring to blend.

APPETIZER fixes fast (see recipe at far left).

Spread 1 teaspoon mixture on each slice of rye bread; sprinkle with oregano. Place on baking sheets; bake at 375° for 15 minutes. Serve hot. (These can be made ahead of time. Allow to cool, then freeze flat on cookie sheets and transfer to heavy freezer bags. To reheat, microwave on 70% power for 1 minute.) **Yield:** about 68 appetizers.

>>>>>>>>※<<<<<<<<<
GREEN CHILI CON QUESO

Marge Wasley, Phoenix, Arizona

1/4 cup butter
1-1/2 cups diced yellow onion
2 garlic cloves, minced
1/2 teaspoon ground pepper
1 can (1 pound) whole tomatoes, drained, seeded and chopped
1 can (4 ounces) chopped green chilies
2 pounds American cheese, cubed
1 jar (5 ounces) cheese spread

Melt butter in a large heavy saucepan or skillet. Add onion, garlic and pepper; saute until transparent but not brown. Add tomatoes and chilies. Cook for several minutes, stirring occasionally. Add cheeses, making sure heat is on low to prevent scorching. Stir frequently until cheese melts and mixture is boiling. Serve hot from a fondue pot or chafing dish with corn chips or raw vegetables, or as a sauce over baked potatoes or steamed vegetables. Store, refrigerated, in a tightly covered container or jar.

Her Gingerbread Takes the Cake!

HOME SWEET HOME is much more than a pleasing sentiment for Rose Spires of Minonk, Illinois.

For a holiday cooks' competition, she constructed an elaborate, ornate gingerbread house confection…one that took *110 hours* of exacting baking and building. The time was well-spent—her house took top honors!

"I tested a dozen gingerbread recipes before finding one that held the walls nice and firm," relates Rose, who regularly receives "Best in Show" ribbons at the State Fair. "Then I gathered all the candy ingredients I could think of to complete the scene."

And what a sweet scene it is! "By melting hard candy, I put in a bay window to peek through," she points out. "My frosted Christmas tree and furniture fit right inside the parlor."

There are more morsels to savor still—sugarplum cobblestones… chocolate bar doors…candy cane fence posts strung with licorice twists. A richly glazed gazebo is latticed with icing, while marzipan reindeer graze leisurely beside it.

In fact, every beam, brick and shingle of Rose's incredible house is deliciously edible! And there's a sweetheart of a story to some other portions.

"My husband, Charles, has a good eye for design," Rose notes. "So he gave me a hand with the

❧
"I can be quick with cake—but not gingerbread!"

floor plan. Plus he built a plywood base to fit the house's foundation.

"Then, when I was all done, he hooked up the house's electricity —so it would shine both inside and out!"

This active farm wife's bent for baking has shone for years now. "Charles (who grows corn and soybeans) and our two daughters always ask for *homemade* birthday cakes," Rose smiles. "And our neighbors know they can count on me to come up with wedding and anniversary cakes, even when they're rush orders.

"But when it comes to making

gingerbread, I take my time!"

That slow-and-easy approach includes a good deal of up-close local research. "Before I baked my first house," Rose recalls, "I toured a number of old homesteads near our farm. "I want my cakes to look as realistic as they are good to eat!"

Insisting on authenticity can have its amusing moments also, she grins—especially on the Spireses' acres!

"One time, I was decorating a cake with a wildlife theme. But no matter how hard I tried, I couldn't seem to get the birds' feathers quite right.

"Charles must have sensed I was getting frustrated. The next thing I knew, he was walking into the living room…carrying a quail from our barnyard! Studying its markings for just a minute was all I needed to solve that problem."

Her husband's *always* happy to offer help like that. He knows that —especially when Christmas is coming—construction season could start at almost any time for his gingerbread house-baking wife!

TASTY DECOR streams from Rose Spires' pastry tube. Her gingerbread architecture (right) won sweet award!

FAMILY FAVORITES

FLAVORFUL, FAST quick breads! They're a savory side dish, guaranteed to satisfy that craving for something warm and homemade on a cold winter's day. And most of them can be stirred up and table-ready in an hour or less!

Clockwise from top: **Butter Dips**, from Elaine Norton, Lansing, Michigan; **Pumpkin Ribbon Bread**, from Cathy Van Sickle, Kokomo, Indiana; **Apple Streusel Muffins**, from Cynthia Kolberg, Syracuse, Indiana; **Almond Tea Bread**, from Kathleen Showers, Briggsdale, Colorado.

These recipes can be found on page 29.

HOME-BAKED GIFT BREADS

GUESSING at what gifts to give? Look no further! Especially in this day of fast-food fads, nothing can compare with home-baked gifts from a country kitchen. They make such a personal gift.

You'll find palate-pleasing recipes to tempt every set of taste buds—from rich, fruit-and-nut breads to light, airy cream scones.

Package a handsome, fiber-rich Bran or Apple Pecan Coffee Cake in a reclaimed holiday tin. Bake miniature fruit and nut breads and wrap for school bus driver, mail carrier or next-door neighbor.

Several of these treats have accompanying spreads. Fill pretty jars (labeled for refrigerator storage) with them…then tie with holiday ribbons.

Clockwise from lower left: **Crunchy Bran Coffee Cake**, Gay Snyder, Stow, Ohio; **Lemon Bread**, Caryn Wiggins, Columbus, Indiana; **Apricot Bread/ Spread**, Bev Bosveld, Waupun, Wisconsin; **Strawberry Nut Bread/ Spread**, Maxine Davidson, Waynoka, Oklahoma; **Apple Pecan Coffee Cake**, Ethel Hodges, Emporia, Kansas; **Poppy Seed Bread**, Tammy Flynn, Broken Bow, Nebraska; **Dark Fruit Bread**, Lonna Pugh, Grandville, Michigan; **Cream Scones**/**Lemon Curd**, Dorothy Child, Malone, New York.

These recipes can be found on pages 26-27.

HOLIDAY HOSPITALITY

HURRAY for holiday entertaining! Polish the pewter, deck the halls and set out a tempting array for a family gathering or neighborhood open house!

The appealing buffet dishes here are favorites for festive meals and sure to make your holidays even more enjoyable.

Begin with appetizers...a tasty shrimp curry dip with colorful crudites...hot cheese snack crackers studded with ripe olives...or a savory cheddar cheese spread.

Round out the feast with a rich seafood chowder, a jeweled cranberry mold and a refreshing holiday fruit salad. And, for an ambrosial ending, bring on the creamy Scandinavian rice pudding!

Counter-clockwise from lower right: **Shrimp Curry Dip**, from Bob Fithian, Fountain Hills, Arizona; **Wisconsin Cheddar Cheese Spread**, from Patricia Hazen, Brookfield, Wisconsin; **Creamy Rice Pudding**, Jeanette Mortenson, Albert Lea, Minnesota; **Cranberry Supreme Salad**, Gertrude Zelepuza, Aberdeen, Washington; **Salmon Chowder**, Linda Fox, Soldotna, Alaska; **Oyster Chowder**, Beverly J. Anderson, Sinclairville, New York; **Holiday Fruit Salad**, from Margaret Wagner Allen, Abingdon, Virginia; **Wheat/Cheese Snack Crackers**, Rosemarie Starr, Hillman, Minnesota.

These recipes can be found on pages 27-28.

⇒⇒⇒⇒⇒⇒⇒❋⇐⇐⇐⇐⇐⇐⇐

CRUNCHY BRAN COFFEE CAKE

Gay Snyder, Stow, Ohio

1-1/4 cups boiling water
1 cup 100% *or* unprocessed bran
1/2 cup butter
1/2 cup sugar
1/2 cup packed brown sugar
2 eggs
1 teaspoon vanilla extract
1 teaspoon baking soda
1 teaspoon cinnamon
1/4 teaspoon salt
1-1/4 cups all-purpose flour
TOPPING:
3 tablespoons butter, melted
1/4 cup 100% bran
1/4 cup packed brown sugar
1/2 cup broken walnuts *or* rolled oats

Combine boiling water and bran in small bowl; let stand for 2-3 minutes. In another bowl, cream together butter and sugars until light and fluffy. Add eggs, one at a time, beating after each addition; add vanilla. In another bowl, combine soda, cinnamon, salt and flour; mix into the creamed mixture until blended. Add bran mixture; stir to blend. Pour into a greased 9-in. round cake pan or 8-in. square pan. Bake at 350° for 30-40 minutes. Combine topping ingredients; set aside. Remove coffee cake from oven; sprinkle topping over all. Broil 2-3 minutes until bubbly. **Yield:** 10 servings.

⇒⇒⇒⇒⇒⇒⇒❋⇐⇐⇐⇐⇐⇐⇐

LEMON BREAD

Caryn Wiggins, Columbus, Indiana

BREAD:
1 cup butter
2 cups sugar
4 eggs
1/2 teaspoon salt
1/2 teaspoon baking soda
3 cups all-purpose flour
1 cup buttermilk
Grated rind of 1 lemon *or* 1
tablespoon lemon peel spice
1 cup finely chopped pecans
GLAZE:
Juice from 2 lemons *or* 1/4 cup lemon juice
1 cup confectioners' sugar

Cream together butter and sugar in mixing bowl on high speed. Blend in eggs, one at a time, beating after each addition. In another bowl, combine salt, soda and flour; add to creamed mixture alternately with buttermilk. Stir in lemon peel and nuts by hand. Grease and flour one

9-in. x 5-in. loaf pan or two 7-in. x 3-in. pans. Then line bottom with parchment paper or waxed paper. Spoon batter into pan(s) and bake at 300° for 80 minutes or until bread tests done with wooden pick. Let bread cool in pan(s) for 10 minutes; remove to cooling racks. Combine glaze ingredients; punch holes in bread with toothpick while still warm. Pour glaze slowly over bread. Cool completely before slicing.

⇒⇒⇒⇒⇒⇒⇒❋⇐⇐⇐⇐⇐⇐⇐

STRAWBERRY NUT BREAD

Maxine Davidson, Waynoka, Oklahoma

1 cup butter
1-1/2 cups sugar
1 teaspoon vanilla extract
1/4 teaspoon lemon extract
4 eggs
3 cups all-purpose flour
1 teaspoon salt
1 teaspoon cream of tartar
1/2 teaspoon baking soda
1 cup strawberry jam (freezer jam works well)
1/2 cup cultured sour cream
1/2 cup broken walnuts
STRAWBERRY SPREAD:
1 package (3 ounces) cream cheese, softened
2 tablespoons strawberry jam

Cream butter, sugar and extracts together in a large bowl until light and fluffy. Add eggs, one at a time, beating well after each addition. In another bowl, sift together flour, salt, cream of tartar and baking soda; set aside. In a small bowl, combine jam and sour cream; add to creamed mixture alternately with dry ingredients. Beat until well combined. Stir in nuts. Divide batter among nine greased and floured 4-1/2-in. x 2-1/2-in. loaf pans. Bake at 350° for 50 minutes or until a wooden pick comes out clean. Cool in pans for 10 minutes; remove to cooling rack. Combine spread ingredients and refrigerate until serving. **Yield:** 9 loaves.

FROM YOUR KITCHEN: For a simple gift that's sure to be appreciated by other cooks, write some of your favorite recipes on 3 x 5 cards and tie them together with a ribbon. They make great stocking stuffers, too!

● Bake goodies and give them as gifts in fabric-covered boxes, sewing baskets, tin buckets or in paper bags tied with calico ribbon. Remember to include the recipe.

⇒⇒⇒⇒⇒⇒⇒❋⇐⇐⇐⇐⇐⇐⇐

APPLE PECAN COFFEE CAKE

Ethel Hodges, Emporia, Kansas

CAKE:
1/2 cup vegetable shortening
1/2 cup butter, softened
1-1/2 cups sugar
2 eggs
3 cups all-purpose flour
2 teaspoons baking powder
1 teaspoon baking soda
1/4 teaspoon salt
1-3/4 cups buttermilk
2 medium apples, pared and thinly sliced
TOPPING:
1/2 cup all-purpose flour
1/2 cup sugar
1-1/2 teaspoons cinnamon
3 tablespoons butter
1/2 cup coarsely chopped pecans

Cream shortening and butter in a large bowl. Add sugar gradually, beating until light and fluffy. Add eggs, one at a time, beating well after each addition. In another bowl, combine flour, baking powder, soda and salt; add to creamed mixture alternately with buttermilk. Spoon half of batter into a greased and floured 13-in. x 9-in. baking pan or spoon one quarter of the batter into two 9-in. round cake pans. Arrange apple slices over top; spread with remaining batter. For topping, combine flour, sugar and cinnamon. Cut in butter; stir in the pecans. Sprinkle evenly over batter. Bake at 350° for 45 minutes or until cake tests done with wooden pick. **Yield:** 16 to 20 servings.

⇒⇒⇒⇒⇒⇒⇒❋⇐⇐⇐⇐⇐⇐⇐

APRICOT BREAD

Bev Bosveld, Waupun, Wisconsin

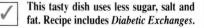 This tasty dish uses less sugar, salt and fat. Recipe includes *Diabetic Exchanges*.

1 cup dried apricots
3/4 cup hot water
2 tablespoons butter, softened
1 cup sugar
1 egg
2 cups all-purpose flour
1 teaspoon baking powder
1/4 teaspoon baking soda
1 teaspoon salt
1/2 cup orange juice
1/2 cup pecans, chopped
APRICOT SPREAD:
1 package (3 ounces) cream cheese, softened
2 tablespoons chopped apricots, softened

Cut apricots into pieces in a small bowl; pour hot water over all. Let soften for 30 minutes. Drain; reserve 1/4 cup apricot water and set aside the apricot pieces. Combine butter, sugar and egg in mixing bowl; cream well. In another bowl, combine flour, baking powder, soda and salt; add to creamed mixture alternately with apricot water and orange juice. Stir in the apricot pieces and pecans. Spoon into a greased and floured 9-in. x 5-in. loaf pan. Bake at 350° for 55-65 minutes or until bread tests done with a wooden pick. For spread, combine cream cheese and apricots; refrigerate until serving. (Bread's flavor improves with age.) **Yield:** 18 slices. **Diabetic Exchanges:** One serving equals 1 bread, 1 fruit, 1 fat; also, 179 calories, 183 mg sodium, 23 mg cholesterol, 30 gm carbohydrate, 3 gm protein, 5 gm fat.

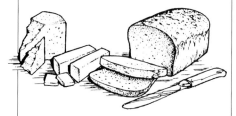

+>+>+>+>+>+>+*<+<+<+<+<+<+<+

POPPY SEED BREAD

Tammy Flynn, Broken Bow, Nebraska

2-1/4 cups sugar
1-1/8 cups vegetable oil
  3 eggs
1-1/2 teaspoons vanilla extract
1-1/2 teaspoons almond extract
1-1/2 teaspoons butter flavor extract
  2 tablespoons poppy seeds
  3 cups all-purpose flour
1-1/2 teaspoons salt
1-1/2 teaspoons baking powder
1-1/2 cups milk
GLAZE:
  1/4 cup orange juice
  1/2 teaspoon vanilla extract
  1/2 teaspoon butter flavor extract
  1/2 teaspoon almond extract
  3/4 cup confectioners' sugar

Combine sugar and oil in a large bowl; beat until blended. Add eggs, one at a time, beating after each addition. Add extracts and poppy seeds; mix well. Set aside. In another bowl, combine the flour, salt and baking powder; add to creamed mixture alternately with milk until well blended. Pour into six 4-1/2-in. x 2-1/2-in. loaf pans, filling one-half to two-thirds full, or miniature pans of choice. Bake at 350° for 45 minutes. Remove from oven; let cool 5 minutes in pans. Combine glaze ingredients; pour over breads while still in pans. Let stand 5 minutes more; remove to cooling rack. **Yield:** 6 small loaves or 10 miniature loaves.

+>+>+>+>+>+>+*<+<+<+<+<+<+<+

DARK FRUIT BREAD

Lonna Pugh, Grandville, Michigan

  1 package (15 ounces) raisins
2-1/4 cups water
  4 tablespoons butter
  2 cups sugar
  2 eggs
  1 teaspoon vanilla extract
  1 package (16 ounces) pitted dates, chopped
5-1/2 cups all-purpose flour, divided
  4 teaspoons baking soda
  1 teaspoon salt
  1 can (20 ounces) crushed pineapple with juice
  1 cup coarsely chopped walnuts
  1 jar (6 ounces) maraschino cherries, halved

In a saucepan (or microwave), boil raisins in water until plumped, about 15 minutes. Drain, reserving about 2/3 to 3/4 cup liquid and setting raisins aside. In a large mixing bowl, cream butter, sugar, eggs and vanilla until fluffy. Add reserved cooled liquid from raisins. In another bowl, combine raisins, dates and 1 cup flour; stir into creamed mixture. Mix remaining flour with baking soda and salt; stir into mixture. Fold in pineapple with juice, nuts and cherries. Fill well-greased tin cans (16- to 20-oz. size) about two-thirds full of batter or four 7-1/2-in. x 3-1/2-in. x 3-in. loaf pans. Bake at 350° for 1 hour. **Yield:** 8 to 9 cans or 4 loaves.

+>+>+>+>+>+>+*<+<+<+<+<+<+<+

CREAM SCONES

Dorothy Child, Malone, New York

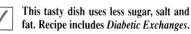

✓ This tasty dish uses less sugar, salt and fat. Recipe includes *Diabetic Exchanges*.

SCONES:
  2 cups all-purpose flour
  3 teaspoons baking powder
  1/2 teaspoon salt
  2 tablespoons sugar
  6 tablespoons butter *or* shortening
  2 eggs
  1/2 cup light cream
  2 tablespoons sugar
LEMON CURD:
  4 tablespoons unsalted butter
  1/2 cup sugar
  1/2 cup fresh lemon juice
  4 egg yolks, slightly beaten
  1 tablespoon grated lemon peel, optional

Combine flour, baking powder, salt and sugar in a medium bowl. Cut in butter or shortening until the mixture resembles coarse crumbs. Set aside. In a small bowl, beat eggs with a fork; add cream. Reserve 2 teaspoons of mixture. Stir remaining egg mixture into flour mixture just until blended. Turn out onto floured board; knead *lightly*. Shape into 14-in. x 7-in. rectangle. Brush with reserved egg mixture. Sprinkle with sugar. Cut into 16 triangular pieces. Place about 1 in. apart on a lightly floured cookie sheet. Bake at 425° for 8-10 minutes. Meanwhile, make lemon curd by combining butter, sugar, lemon juice and egg yolks in a heavy saucepan over low heat (may use double boiler). Stir mixture constantly until it thickens enough to coat back of spoon (soft custard consistency). *Do not boil or mixture will curdle.* Stir in lemon peel, if desired. Pour into jar, seal and refrigerate. Serve warm scones with lemon curd or jam. **Yield:** 16 scones. **Diabetic Exchanges:** One serving equals 1 bread, 1 fruit, 1-1/2 fat; also, 212 calories, 198 mg sodium, 121 mg cholesterol, 23 gm carbohydrate, 4 gm protein, 8 gm fat.

+>+>+>+>+>+>+*<+<+<+<+<+<+<+

CREAMY RICE PUDDING

Jeanette Mortenson, Albert Lea, Minnesota

  6 cups milk
  1 cup long-grain white rice
  1 cup heavy whipping cream
  3 egg yolks, beaten
  2 teaspoons vanilla extract
  1/4 teaspoon salt
  1/2 cup sugar
  1/2 cup raisins, optional
Cinnamon

Combine milk and rice in a heavy saucepan; bring to boil. Reduce heat; simmer for 55 minutes. Combine cream, egg yolks, vanilla, salt and sugar and raisins, if desired; add to rice mixture. Cook over moderate heat, stirring until thick. Pour into 2-1/2-qt. serving dish; sprinkle top with cinnamon. Serve warm, or cover and store in refrigerator. **Yield:** 10 servings.

SUGAR SOFTENER: To restore the moisture to hardened brown sugar, place the sugar in an airtight container together with a large apple slice or a piece of bread. Or, warm sugar in the oven for a few minutes until a soft texture returns; then keep it fresh and moist by storing in a tightly closed bag in the refrigerator.

OYSTER CHOWDER

Beverly J. Anderson, Sinclairville, New York

12 ounces fresh shucked oysters
   with liquid (canned may be
   substituted but omit salt)
1 onion, coarsely chopped
   (about 1/2 cup)
1 medium potato, diced
1 cup coarsely cut broccoli
1/2 cup frozen corn
1 cup water
1/4 cup butter
1/4 cup all-purpose flour
1 cup chicken broth
3 cups milk
Salt and white pepper to taste

Heat oysters in liquid in a pan until edges curl; set aside. In another saucepan, combine onion, potato, broccoli, corn and water; simmer until vegetables are tender. Set aside. Melt butter in a pan, stir in flour. Cook, stirring, for 1 minute. Add broth and milk gradually; cook until mixture thickens. Add reserved oysters and vegetables. Heat through but *do not boil*. Season to taste. **Yield:** 6-8 servings.

WISCONSIN CHEDDAR CHEESE SPREAD

Patricia Hazen, Brookfield, Wisconsin

1 pound sharp cheddar cheese,
   shredded
1 cup chopped walnuts
1 cup mayonnaise
1/4 cup finely diced green onions
1/2 teaspoon curry powder
Dash hot pepper sauce

Combine all ingredients; mix well. Pack into crocks or form into a cheese ball; refrigerate until firm. (Cheese ball can be rolled in chopped nuts or parsley, if desired.) Serve with assorted crackers. **Yield:** 24 servings.

SHRIMP CURRY DIP

Bob Fithian, Fountain Hills, Arizona

1 can (4-1/2 ounces) tiny
   shrimp pieces
1-1/3 cups mayonnaise
1 teaspoon to 1 tablespoon
   honey
2 tablespoons catsup
1 medium onion, finely diced
2 teaspoons lemon juice
1 teaspoon tarragon vinegar
1 to 1-1/2 teaspoons curry
   powder

Dash hot pepper sauce
Salt and pepper to taste
Assorted fresh vegetables
   (broccoli florets, pepper strips,
   carrot sticks, scallions)

Combine all ingredients except vegetables; mix well; refrigerate overnight. Serve cold with vegetables. (This also makes an excellent salad dressing thinned with milk.)

WHEAT/CHEESE SNACK CRACKERS

Rosemarie Starr, Hillman, Minnesota

1 box (13 ounces) shredded
   wheat snack crackers
1-1/2 cups mayonnaise (no
   substitutes)
2 cups (8 ounces) shredded
   mozzarella cheese
2 cups (8 ounces) shredded
   cheddar cheese
1 can (4-1/4 ounces) chopped
   ripe olives
6 green onions, sliced 1/8 inch
   thick

Place crackers, with edges touching, on a cookie sheet. Combine mayonnaise, cheeses, olives and onions; spread on crackers. Bake at 250° for 20 minutes. Serve hot. **Yield:** 5 dozen.

CRANBERRY SUPREME SALAD

Gertrude Zelepuza, Aberdeen, Washington

1 package (3 ounces) raspberry-
   flavored gelatin
2 cups boiling water, *divided*
1 can (16 ounces) whole
   cranberry sauce
1 package (3 ounces) lemon-
   flavored gelatin
1 package (3 ounces) cream
   cheese
1/3 cup mayonnaise
1 can (8-1/2 ounces) crushed
   pineapple with juice
1 cup whipping cream
1 cup miniature marshmallows

Dissolve raspberry gelatin in 1 cup boiling water; stir in cranberry sauce. Pour into bottom of a 1-1/2-qt. round mold. Chill until partially set. Dissolve lemon gelatin in 1 cup boiling water; set aside. Beat together cream cheese and mayonnaise; gradually add lemon gelatin. Stir in pineapple and juice. Chill until partially set. Whip cream; fold into lemon mixture; add marshmallows. Spread lemon layer on top of cranberry layer. Chill until set. **Yield:** 12 servings.

HOLIDAY FRUIT SALAD

Margaret Wagner Allen, Abingdon, Virginia

1 can (15-1/2 ounces) pineapple
   chunks, juice drained and
   reserved
1/2 cup sugar
2 tablespoons all-purpose flour
1 egg, beaten
1 cup pecans, chopped
3 bananas, sliced
2 cans (11 ounces *each*)
   mandarin oranges, drained
3 medium unpeeled apples,
   chopped
1/2 pound red seedless grapes,
   halved

In a small saucepan, combine pineapple juice, sugar, flour and egg; cook over low heat, stirring constantly until smooth and thickened. Cool. Combine pecans and fruit; add dressing and stir well. Chill before serving. **Yield:** 10-12 servings.

PREPARING POINSETTIAS: If you saved your poinsettia from last Christmas, or if you have holiday cactus plants, October is the time to begin getting them ready for the holiday season. The plants need complete darkness for 15 hours each day, such as from 5 p.m. to 8 a.m. During the day they need all the sun they can get, but no artificial light at night. Even a slightly opened door can interrupt the dark period and delay flowering.

SALMON CHOWDER

Linda Fox, Soldotna, Alaska

1 medium onion, chopped
4 tablespoons butter *or*
   margarine
1 cup water
1 package (20 ounces) frozen
   chopped broccoli
1 can (16 ounces) red salmon,
   bones and skin removed
2 teaspoons instant chicken
   bouillon granules
1 can (14-1/2 ounces)
   evaporated milk
2 tablespoons all-purpose flour
4 cups milk
Salt and white pepper to taste

Saute onion in butter in Dutch oven until transparent. Add water and broccoli; simmer until broccoli is tender. Add salmon, bouillon granules, combined evaporated milk and flour, and milk. Season to taste. Heat until chowder thickens slightly. **Yield:** 8 servings.

＋≻≻≻≻≻≻≻※≺≺≺≺≺≺≺≺

PUMPKIN
RIBBON BREAD

Cathy Van Sickle, Kokomo, Indiana

FILLING:
    2 packages (3 ounces *each*)
      cream cheese, softened
  1/3 cup sugar
    1 tablespoon all-purpose flour
    1 egg
    2 teaspoons grated orange peel
BREAD:
    1 cup cooked pumpkin
  1/2 cup vegetable oil
    2 eggs
1-1/2 cups sugar
  1/2 teaspoon salt
  1/2 teaspoon cloves
  1/2 teaspoon cinnamon
1-2/3 cups all-purpose flour
    1 teaspoon baking soda
    1 cup chopped pecans

For filling, beat cream cheese, sugar and flour together in a small bowl. Add egg; mix to blend. Stir in orange peel; set aside. For bread, combine pumpkin, oil and eggs in a large bowl. Add remaining ingredients; mix to blend. Pour one-quarter of batter into two greased and floured 7-1/2-in. x 3-1/2-in. x 3-in. loaf pans. Carefully spread filling over batter. Cover filling with remaining batter. Bake at 325° for 1-1/2 hours or until bread tests done with a wooden pick. Cool 10 minutes before removing from pans. Store in refrigerator.

＋≻≻≻≻≻≻≻※≺≺≺≺≺≺≺≺

APPLE STREUSEL
MUFFINS

Cynthia Kolberg, Syracuse, Indiana

 This tasty dish uses less sugar, salt and fat. Recipe includes *Diabetic Exchanges*.

1-1/2 cups all-purpose flour
  1/4 cup sugar
    2 teaspoons baking powder
  1/2 teaspoon cinnamon
  1/4 teaspoon salt
  1/8 teaspoon nutmeg
    1 cup pared shredded apple
  1/2 cup milk
  1/4 cup vegetable oil
    1 egg, beaten
STREUSEL:
  1/3 cup packed brown sugar
    2 tablespoons all-purpose flour
  1/2 teaspoon cinnamon
    2 tablespoons butter, softened
  1/3 cup chopped pecans

In a medium bowl, sift together flour, sugar, baking powder, cinnamon, salt and nutmeg. Stir in apple; set aside. In a small bowl, combine milk, oil and egg until blended; add to dry ingredients; stir just until moistened. Spoon half of batter into 12 greased muffin cups. For streusel, combine all ingredients. Reserve 3 tablespoons; sprinkle remaining on top of batter. Fill each cup with remaining batter, then top with remaining streusel. Bake at 400° for 20-25 minutes or until muffins test done with a wooden pick. Serve warm. (To make bread, use an 8-in. x 8-in. x 4-in. loaf pan and bake at 350° for 45-50 minutes. Cool in pan for 10 minutes before removing to wire rack.) **Yield:** 12 muffins or 1 loaf. **Diabetic Exchanges:** One serving equals 1 bread, 1 fruit, 1-1/2 fat; also, 193 calories, 149 mg sodium, 28 mg cholesterol, 25 gm carbohydrate, 3 gm protein, 8 gm fat.

＋≻≻≻≻≻≻≻※≺≺≺≺≺≺≺≺

ALMOND TEA BREAD

Kathleen Showers, Briggsdale, Colorado

    1 can (8 ounces) almond paste
  1/4 cup butter, softened
    1 cup sugar
    3 eggs
1-1/2 cups pitted cherries *or*
      blueberries
    3 cups all-purpose flour,
      divided
    4 teaspoons baking powder
  1/2 teaspoon salt
  3/4 cup milk

In a large bowl, combine almond paste and butter; beat until well blended. Gradually add sugar, beating until light and fluffy. Add eggs, one at a time, beating well after each addition. Set aside. Combine cherries or blueberries and 1 tablespoon flour; toss gently to coat. In another bowl, combine remaining flour with baking powder and salt; add to creamed mixture alternately with milk. Spoon one-sixth of batter into two greased and floured 7-1/2-in. x 3-1/2-in. x 3-in. loaf pans; top with half of fruit. Repeat layers. Spoon remaining batter on top; smooth with spatula. Bake at 350° for 1 hour and 15 minutes or until bread tests done with a wooden pick. Cool in pan 10 minutes; remove to a wire rack.

＋≻≻≻≻≻≻≻※≺≺≺≺≺≺≺≺

BUTTER DIPS

Elaine Norton, Lansing, Michigan

  1/3 cup butter
2-1/2 cups all-purpose flour
    1 tablespoon sugar
3-1/2 teaspoons baking powder

1-1/2 teaspoons salt
  1/2 to 1 cup shredded sharp
      cheddar cheese
    1 cup milk
**Sesame seeds *or* garlic, onion *or*
  celery salt***

Place butter in a 13-in. x 9-in. x 2-in. baking pan; melt in a 450° oven. Remove from oven and set aside. In a large bowl, combine flour, sugar, baking powder, salt and cheese. Add milk; stir slowly with a fork. When dough clings together, turn onto a well-floured board. Roll to coat with flour; knead gently 10 times. Roll dough into a 12-in. x 8-in. rectangle, 1/2 in. thick. With a sharp knife, cut dough in half, then into 16 strips. Dip both sides of sticks in butter. Lay two rows in pan. Sprinkle with sesame seeds or garlic, onion or celery salt. (*Garlic, onion or celery powder can be substituted to reduce sodium.) Bake at 450° for 12-15 minutes. Serve immediately. **Yield:** 32 sticks.

＋≻≻≻≻≻≻≻※≺≺≺≺≺≺≺≺

RASPBERRY CREAM
CHEESE COFFEE CAKE

LaVonne Cunningham, Colfax, Illinois

(Not Pictured)

    1 package (3 ounces) cream
      cheese
    3 tablespoons butter
    2 cups biscuit mix
  1/3 cup milk
  1/2 to 3/4 cup raspberry jam *or*
      preserves
Slivered almonds
GLAZE:
    1 cup confectioners' sugar
    2 tablespoons milk
Dab of butter

In a large bowl, cut cream cheese and butter into biscuit mix until crumbly. Mix in milk. Turn onto a large sheet of waxed paper; pat down. Lay another sheet of waxed paper over top. Roll dough between paper into a large rectangle. Pull off top paper and turn dough onto a lightly greased baking sheet. Remove other sheet of paper; spread jam down center of dough. Slit sides at 1-in. intervals and fold strips over filling. Bake at 425° for 12-15 minutes. Combine glaze ingredients until creamy; drizzle over cake. Sprinkle the almonds on top.

▲ ▲ A YULETIDE BUFFET ▲ ▲

PULL UP a chair and join us—it's time for holiday feasting with family and friends! Our table is decked out with dishes that provide refreshing new twists on traditional favorites.

Pique your appetite with spicy, Mississippi-style baked shrimp, or the fresh flavors and festive colors of pickled mushrooms. Serve up a crispy brown roasted duckling, but instead of the usual bread stuffing, try our pleasant brown rice/pecan variation.

Accompany it with acorn squash, baked with an intriguing and flavorful filling of hot Italian sausage and maple syrup. And save room to savor the tart contrasts of a colorful and unusual salad of avocado and pink grapefruit. Round out the feast with colorful, apple-studded red cabbage, a cranberry salad liberally laced with orange, and flavorful, feather-light sourdough rolls.

Clockwise from lower left: **Avocado/Grapefruit Salad**, from Caroline Weiler, Sarasota, Florida; (on same plate) **Sourdough Butterflake Refrigerator Rolls**, from Kalli Deschamps, Missoula, Montana; **Pickled Mushrooms**, Mavis Diment, Marcus, Iowa; **Renaissance Red Cabbage**, Angela Biggin, LaGrange Park, Illinois; **Duck with Brown Rice Stuffing**, from Nancy Brissey, Auburn, Washington; **Baked Squash with Sausage**, Donie Kaup, Albion, Nebraska; **Fresh Cranberry Salad**, from Cathy Burke, Oneida, Tennessee; **Biloxi-Style Appetizer Shrimp**, from Diane Hixon, Niceville, Florida.

These recipes can be found on pages 33-34.

☃ DESSERT DELIGHTS ☃

LEAVE ROOM for dessert—especially when the buffet boasts these spectacular treats!

Sink your fork into a rich and smooth classic cheesecake …or a light, almond-studded chocolate torte with a whipped cream filling. Spoon up some buttery fresh cranberry topping or a cool coffee-flavored ice cream pie. Can't decide? Try them all!

Clockwise from lower left: **Mississippi Mud Pie**, Sara Carley, Temple, New Hampshire; **Ultimate Cheesecake**, Cathy Burke, Oneida, Tennessee; **Chocolate Torte**, Rose M. Johnson, Virginia, Minnesota; **Cranberry Topping**, Kristi Twohig, Fond du Lac, Wis.

These recipes can be found on pages 34-35.

RENAISSANCE RED CABBAGE

Angela Biggin, La Grange Park, Illinois

> 1 head red cabbage (about 5 pounds)
> 1 cup dry red wine *or* unsweetened apple juice
> 3 tablespoons white *or* apple cider vinegar
> 1/4 teaspoon salt
> 1/8 teaspoon ground pepper
> 1/8 teaspoon ground cloves
> 2 teaspoons ground cinnamon
> 2 whole bay leaves
> 3 tablespoons sugar
> 5 tablespoons whole *or* jellied cranberry sauce
> 2 cooking apples, peeled and cut into 1/2-inch cubes
> 1/2 cup sweetened applesauce

Shred cabbage in food processor or by hand. Combine with wine and vinegar in a large kettle. Cover; bring to boil. Reduce heat to low; cook about 5 minutes. Add salt, pepper, cloves, cinnamon, bay leaves, sugar, cranberry sauce and apples. Cook about 20 minutes. Add applesauce. Remove bay leaves before serving. Serve with roast pork or duck. **Yield:** 16-20 servings.

AVOCADO/GRAPEFRUIT SALAD

Caroline Weiler, Sarasota, Florida

> 2 ripe avocados, peeled, pitted and sliced lengthwise into 1/4-inch slices
> 2 large red grapefruit, peeled and sectioned with white membrane removed
> Boston lettuce leaves, washed and chilled

POPPY SEED DRESSING:
> 1/3 cup sugar
> 1 teaspoon dry mustard
> 5 tablespoons vinegar
> 1 teaspoon salt
> 1 cup vegetable oil
> 1-1/2 teaspoons grated onion, drained on paper towel
> 2-1/2 teaspoons poppy seeds

Arrange several slices of avocado and grapefruit on a bed of lettuce, alternating slices for color; chill. Make dressing by mixing sugar, mustard, vinegar and salt. Slowly add oil, beating vigorously between additions (dressing will be very thick). Stir in onion and poppy seeds. Spoon on salads and serve immediately. **Yield:** 8 servings.

PICKLED MUSHROOMS

Mavis Diment, Marcus, Iowa

> 2 pounds fresh mushrooms
> 1/2 cup olive oil
> 1/4 cup lemon juice
> 1/4 cup water
> 1 teaspoon minced garlic
> 3/4 teaspoon salt
> 1/2 teaspoon salt
> 1/2 teaspoon pepper
> 1/3 cup chopped fresh parsley
> 1/4 cup diced sweet red pepper

Place washed mushrooms in a glass serving bowl; set aside. Mix oil, lemon, juice, water, garlic, salt and pepper in saucepan and bring to a boil. Pour over mushrooms. Cover; refrigerate for at least 2 hours. Stir in parsley and pepper. **Yield:** 10 appetizer servings.

SOURDOUGH BUTTERFLAKE REFRIGERATOR ROLLS

Kalli Deschamps, Missoula, Montana

SOURDOUGH STARTER:
(NOTE: Starter must be made 2-3 days in advance.)
> 2 cups all-purpose flour
> 1 teaspoon salt
> 3 tablespoons sugar
> 1 tablespoon dry yeast
> 2 cups lukewarm water

Stir together flour, salt, sugar and yeast with wooden spoon in large mixing bowl; gradually add lukewarm water. Stir until mixture resembles a smooth paste. Cover with towel or cheesecloth; set in warm (85°) place. Stir mixture several times a day. Store in a heavy plastic container with air hole. It will be ready in 2-3 days.

SOURDOUGH REFRIGERATOR ROLLS:
(NOTE: Dough must "rest" overnight.)
> 2 packages dry yeast
> 1/3 cup warm water (110°)
> 1 cup sourdough starter (recipe above)
> 1/2 cup vegetable oil
> 3 eggs, well beaten
> 1 cup warm water
> 1/2 cup sugar
> 1 teaspoon salt
> 5-1/2 to 6-1/2 cups all-purpose flour, *divided*
> 1/4 cup butter, melted

Soften yeast in 1/3 cup warm water; set aside. In a large mixing bowl, combine the starter, oil, eggs, 1 cup warm water, sugar, salt and 2 cups flour. Stir vigorously for 1 minute. Stir in softened yeast

and enough flour to make dough that pulls away from sides of bowl. Cover with cloth; set in warm, draft-free place to let rise until doubled. Punch down; cover with plastic wrap. Refrigerate overnight. Three hours before baking, roll out dough on lightly floured surface to a 1/4-in. to 1/2-in. thick rectangle, about 7 in. wide and 26 in. long. Brush with butter. Starting with long side, roll up jelly-roll style. Cut into 1-in. slices. Place in greased muffin pans, cut side down. Cover with cloth. Let rise until doubled, about 2-1/2 hours. Bake at 400° for 12-15 minutes until golden brown. **Yield:** 2-1/2 dozen.

BILOXI-STYLE APPETIZER SHRIMP

Diane Hixon, Niceville, Florida

> 1 bag shrimp and crab boil
> 2 cans (12 ounces *each*) beer *or* 24 ounces water
> 1 tablespoon hot pepper sauce
> 1 tablespoon Worcestershire sauce
> 1 teaspoon salt
> 1/2 teaspoon garlic powder
> Pepper to taste
> 3 tablespoons fresh lemon *or* lime juice
> 5 pounds fresh medium shrimp, shelled and deveined
> 1 cup unsalted butter, melted

Bring spice bag to boil in beer or water in a large saucepan. Add the hot pepper and Worcestershire sauces, salt, garlic powder, pepper and lemon or lime juice. Simmer for 10 minutes to blend flavors. Arrange shrimp in an ovenproof casserole; pour liquid over them. Pour melted butter over all. Bake at 350° for 15 minutes, stirring twice. **Yield:** 20 appetizer servings.

CURLY CRUDITES: For easy holiday hors d'oeuvres, place thin carrot strips and radish rosettes in ice water and watch them curl! Then arrange them on a serving platter with some vegetable dip.

DUCK WITH BROWN RICE STUFFING

Nancy Brissey, Auburn, Washington

**1 duckling (about 5 pounds),
    rinsed and dried**
STUFFING:
    1 cup brown rice
    2 cups chicken stock
    **1 cup sliced green onions and
        tops**
    1 cup diced celery
    1/2 cup butter
    **5 to 6 ounces (1-1/2 cups) sliced
        fresh mushrooms**
    1 teaspoon salt
    **1 cup pecan pieces (1/4-inch
        pieces)**

Cook rice in chicken stock in a covered heavy saucepan until liquid is absorbed, about 40 minutes. While rice is cooking, saute green onions and celery in butter until vegetables are tender. Add mushrooms and saute about 5 minutes. Stir in salt, cooked rice and pecan pieces. Stuff duck. Preheat oven to 450°. Place duck in roasting pan; immediately lower temperature to 350° and roast, uncovered, until tender, allowing about 25 minutes per pound. Allow to rest for 10 minutes before carving. **Yield:** 4 servings.

ULTIMATE CHEESECAKE

Cathy Burke, Oneida, Tennessee

CRUST:
    1 cup all-purpose flour
    1/4 cup sugar
    1 teaspoon grated lemon peel
    1/2 teaspoon vanilla extract
    1 egg yolk
    1/4 cup butter, softened
FILLING:
    **5 packages (8 ounces *each*)
        cream cheese, softened**
    1-1/4 cups sugar
    3 tablespoons all-purpose flour
    1/4 teaspoon vanilla extract
    5 eggs
    2 egg yolks
    1/4 cup whipping cream
    2 teaspoons grated lemon peel
    1-1/2 teaspoons grated orange peel
GLAZE:
    2 tablespoons sugar
    4 teaspoons cornstarch
    **2 cans (8 ounces *each*) crushed
        pineapple, undrained**
    2 teaspoons lemon juice
    1 perfect strawberry for garnish

Make crust by mixing all ingredients until blended. Pat half of the crust mixture on bottom of greased 9-in. springform pan (sides of the pan should be *well-greased* as well). Bake at 400° until golden brown, about 6-8 minutes; cool. Press the rest of dough onto sides of pan; set aside. Make filling by mixing cheese, sugar, flour and vanilla at high speed. Add eggs and yolks one at a time, beating well after each addition. Beat in the cream; stir in the grated peels. Pour into assembled springform pan; bake at 500° for 10 minutes. Lower oven temperature to 250°; bake for 1 hour. Remove to rack to cool for at least 2 hours. Refrigerate. For glaze, mix sugar and cornstarch; add pineapple and lemon juice. Bring to boil over medium heat. Cook for 1 minute until thick. Cool; top the cooled cheesecake with glaze. Chill for at least 3 hours (overnight is best). Remove sides of pan; garnish with a single strawberry.

MISSISSIPPI MUD PIE

Sara W. Carley, Temple, New Hampshire

CRUST:
    **24 chocolate wafers, mashed fine
        (about 1-1/3 cups), *divided***
    **3 tablespoons butter *or*
        margarine, softened**
FILLING:
    **1/2 gallon coffee ice cream,
        softened**
HOT FUDGE SAUCE:
    **2 ounces (2 squares)
        unsweetened chocolate**
    1/2 cup water
    1-1/2 cups light corn syrup
    1/8 teaspoon salt
    1 teaspoon vanilla extract
WHIPPED CREAM TOPPING:
    1 cup whipping cream
    1 tablespoon sugar
    1 teaspoon vanilla extract

For crust, combine crumbs and butter. Set aside 3 tablespoons for garnish; press remaining into bottom and sides of 9-in. pie plate. Bake at 375° for 8 minutes; cool. Pack softened ice cream into the cooled crust. Freeze until firm. For sauce, melt chocolate with water in saucepan over low heat until blended. Remove from heat; gradually add syrup and salt. Bring to boil; reduce heat and simmer for 10 minutes, stirring often. Add vanilla; set aside. For topping, whip cream; add sugar and vanilla. To serve, cut pie into wedges, place on dessert plates, pour fudge sauce over, top with whipped cream and sprinkle with reserved crumbs. **Yield:** 8 servings.

FRESH CRANBERRY SALAD

Cathy Burke, Oneida, Tennessee

    **1 package (12 ounces) fresh
        cranberries, washed and sorted**
1-1/2 cups sugar
    **3 packages (3 ounces *each*)
        orange-flavored gelatin**
    3 cups boiling water
    **2 cans (11 ounces *each*)
        mandarin oranges, drained
        and cut in small pieces**
    **1 cup chopped walnuts *or*
        pecans**
    **1 can (8 ounces) crushed
        pineapple, undrained**

Grind cranberries in a food grinder or food processor; stir in sugar. Set aside. Dissolve gelatin in water; cool until mixture begins to thicken. Combine with cranberry mixture. Add oranges, nuts and pineapple. Stir well; pour into lightly greased 8-cup mold. Chill overnight. Unmold and serve on plate of greens. **Yield:** 16 servings.

BAKED SQUASH WITH SAUSAGE

Donie Kaup, Albion, Nebraska

    2 small acorn squash
    4 tablespoons pure maple syrup
    2 tablespoons butter
    **8 ounces bulk hot Italian
        sausage**

Cut squash in half; clean the seeds out. Spoon a fourth of the maple syrup, butter and sausage into each cavity. Place squash on baking sheet. Bake at 350° for 30-40 minutes or until fork-tender. **Yield:** 4 servings.

SPICY SCENTS: Let the fragrance of Christmas drift through the house. Put 3 cups of water in a pot, add a tablespoon of whole cloves plus two or three sticks of cinnamon, a few citrus peels, and a teaspoon each of ground nutmeg and ground ginger. Bring mixture to a boil, then let it simmer on stove on low.

CHOCOLATE TORTE

Rose M. Johnson, Virginia, Minnesota

TORTE:
- 8 eggs, *separated*
- 1-1/4 cups sugar
- 3/4 cup all-purpose flour
- 1/4 cup fine dry bread crumbs
- 1/4 teaspoon salt
- 2 ounces (2 squares) semisweet chocolate, grated
- 1-1/2 teaspoons vanilla extract

CREAM FILLING:
- 1/2 cup whipping cream
- 1/4 cup ground almonds
- 3 tablespoons sugar

FROSTING:
- 4 ounces (4 squares) unsweetened chocolate
- 3 tablespoons butter
- 1 tablespoon brandy *or* 1 teaspoon vanilla extract
- 2 to 2-1/2 cups confectioners' sugar
- 2 to 3 tablespoons milk
- Chopped almonds for garnish

Beat the egg yolks until thick and lemon-colored. Gradually beat in the sugar; set aside. Combine flour, bread crumbs and salt. Add chocolate and mix thoroughly, but lightly; add to yolk/sugar mixture in 4 portions, folding until well mixed after each addition. Set aside. With clean beaters, beat egg whites with vanilla until stiff, but not dry, peaks are formed. Stir 1 cup of egg whites into batter (makes batter less stiff for folding). Gently fold in remaining egg whites. Turn into a well-greased and parchment-lined 9- or 10-in. springform pan or deep, round layer cake pan. (Torte in photo was baked in 8-in. pan.) Bake at 325° for 50-60 minutes. Remove from pan; cool completely. Split cake in half. Set aside. Make filling by whipping cream, then folding in almonds and sugar. Spread filling on bottom half of cake. Replace top. For frosting, melt chocolate and butter in saucepan; remove from heat. Stir in brandy or vanilla; add sugar and milk, mixing until frosting is of spreading consistency. (Work quickly as frosting sets up fast.) Frost sides and top of cake. Press the chopped almonds around sides of cake. Refrigerate for 4 hours or longer to let the flavors mellow. **Yield:** 20 servings.

CRANBERRY TOPPING

Kristi Twohig, Fond du Lac, Wisconsin

- 1/2 cup butter
- 1 cup white *or* brown sugar
- 1 package (12 ounces) whole cranberries, washed and sorted
- 1/2 cup orange-flavored liqueur *or* orange juice concentrate
- 1/2 cup whipping cream, optional

Combine butter, sugar, cranberries and liqueur or concentrate. Bring to boil over medium heat, stirring constantly. Reduce heat; simmer until berries pop. Remove from heat; stir in cream, if desired. Serve warm or at room temperature over pound cake, cheesecake or ice cream. Makes a nice Christmas gift (be sure to include instructions to store in refrigerator). **Yield:** 4 cups.

BANANA BRAN MUFFINS

Sue Gillard, Carnation, Washington

(Not Pictured)

- 1/2 cup butter
- 1/2 cup packed brown sugar
- 3 bananas, mashed
- 1/4 cup milk
- 1 teaspoon vanilla extract
- 2 eggs
- 1-1/2 cups all-purpose flour
- 1/2 cup unprocessed bran
- 1 teaspoon baking powder
- 1 teaspoon baking soda
- 1/4 teaspoon salt
- 1 cup chopped walnuts

In a large bowl, cream the butter and brown sugar until fluffy. Add bananas, milk, vanilla and eggs; blend well. Stir in flour, bran, baking powder, soda and salt; blend just until dry ingredients are moistened. Stir in walnuts. Spoon into 12 greased muffin cups. Bake at 375° for 20-25 minutes. Cool 5 minutes before removing from cups. **Yield:** 12 muffins.

CHRISTMAS CUBES: To make festive ice cubes for cool drinks, fill ice cube trays halfway with water. Float a washed holly leaf, wild violet, mint leaf, olive or similar item on top and freeze. Then fill trays to the top and freeze again. This traps the object in the center of the cube. They'd look particularly pretty floating in a punch bowl for a special occasion. For convenience, make them ahead of time and store in a zip-top bag in the freezer.

SAVORY CHEESE BREADSTICKS

Jane Haines, Arcadia, Wisconsin

(Not Pictured)

- 2 cups all-purpose flour
- 1 tablespoon baking powder
- 1/2 teaspoon salt
- 1/2 teaspoon Italian seasoning*
- 1 cup (4 ounces) shredded sharp cheddar cheese
- 2/3 cup milk
- 1/3 cup unsalted butter, melted
- 1 egg
- 1 teaspoon water

In a medium bowl, combine flour, baking powder, salt, Italian seasoning (*1/8 teaspoon *each* oregano, marjoram, basil and sage may be substituted), cheese, milk and butter. Stir until mixture no longer sticks to bowl (about 2-3 minutes). Turn dough out onto a floured surface and knead lightly 10 times. Divide into 24 equal pieces. Roll each into a 6-in. rope. Twist two ropes together; press lightly at ends. Repeat with remaining dough. Place on a greased cookie sheet. Beat egg with water; brush on breadsticks. Bake at 400° for 12-17 minutes or until light golden brown. Remove from cookie sheet immediately. Serve warm. **Yield:** 12 breadsticks.

Collection Is Cookie Cut Above!

By Susan Davis
Sterling, Colorado

PICK a shape—any shape—and you're likely going to find it in Elenna Firme's cookie cutter collection...she has more than 3,000 to choose from!

But if you can't find just the right cutter to shape a sweet snack, don't worry. This Haxtun, Colorado baker gladly will make one for you.

Cookies and cutters have been a happy hobby for Elenna since 1980, when her husband's grandmother gave her her first set of cutters.

"She also gave me the address of a club for cookie cutter collectors," Elenna adds with a grin. "One thing led to another...and before long, my kitchen was cluttered with cutters!"

A whole-wall display cured that cutter clutter. But as Elenna's sons, Daniel and Matthew, grew, so did her collection.

"They did outgrow the Mother Goose and Sesame Street cookies I was making for them and started asking for baseball players, astronauts and robots instead," Elenna explains. "When I couldn't find the cutters they wanted, I decided to make them myself!"

Elenna's first homemade cutters were a big success with her little cookie-munchers, who challenged her with requests for *other* shapes. And she hasn't cut out cutting them out yet.

"First, I draw my ideas on paper," Elenna says. "Not *everything* makes a nice cookie cutter. I buy food-safe tin in sheets," she continues, "and I use tin snips,

🎄 "I enjoy the challenge of making new cutters!"

Vise-Grips and pliers for cutting and shaping it."

When the cutter is shaped, Elenna solders both the inside and outside edges of the seams so it can't pull apart. The amount of time it takes to complete a cutter varies depending on the complexity of the design. An old-fashioned bonnet may take only 10 minutes, but an intricate animal shape takes half an hour or more.

Elenna delights in adding special touches to each cutter, whether it's a twist to a lamb's tail or a flourish of feathers on a turkey. "That extra detail is what makes a cutter unique, unlike anybody else's," she notes.

Elenna's unique cookie cutters have caught the eyes of other collectors, who often ask her to make cutters for them.

Recently, volunteers from Wyoming's state museum wrote requesting a cutter copy of the state capitol building, in honor of Wyoming's centennial celebration. They were so pleased when they saw her design that they ordered 75 more cutters!

That request and others keep Elenna busy bending and baking. "I enjoy the challenge of making new cutters," she says enthusiastically.

Judging by her kitchen creations, it's clear she's cut out for the job!

If you would like Elenna to make a special cutter for you (for a fee), write to her at 42795 County Road 15, Haxtun CO 80731. Elenna asks that you please include a self-addressed stamped envelope.

COOKIE CREATIONS. Elenna Firme bends and shapes cutters, creating new cookie shapes and large cutter collection!

COUNTRY CONFECTIONS

IN country kitchens, celebrating Christmas means many things—foremost among them festive candy!

As a tasty treat for family and friends, or gaily wrapped for gift-giving, homemade holiday sweets satisfy in the form of easy microwave candies...flavorful fruit...elegant hand-dipped chocolates—plus everything in between. From the scrumptious collection of luscious goodies shown here and on the next two pages... you'll find a complete sweet-tooth-satisfying guide for the holidays. It's the best of the season...all for you!

Clockwise from top of photo: **Aunt Rose's Fantastic Butter Toffee**, from Rosie Kimberlin, Los Angeles, California; **Macadamia Nut Fudge**, from Vicki Fioranelli, Cleveland, Mississippi; **Mounds Balls**, Kathy Dorman, Snover, Michigan; **Easy Microwave Caramels**, from Darleen Worm, Fond du Lac, Wisconsin.

These recipes can be found on page 40.

SEASON'S SWEETS

Clockwise from lower left: **Orange Sugared Pecans**, from Murri Mills, Brady, Texas; **Stuffed Dates**, Dorothy Pepper, Thermal, California; **Chocolate Almond Truffles**, Arla Railsback, New Richmond, Wisconsin; **Two-Tone Fudge**, Lavonne Sullivan, Topeka, Kansas; **Microwave Leche Quemada**, Mildred Kneupper, New Braunfels, Texas; **Spiced Mixed Nuts**, Joanne Warner, Baldwin, Wisconsin; **Orange/Chocolate Sugarplums**, from Evelyn Skaggs, Nixa, Missouri; **Candied Citrus Peels**, from Mary Malinowski, Lee Center, New York.

These recipes can be found on pages 40-41.

AUNT ROSE'S FANTASTIC BUTTER TOFFEE

Rosie Kimberlin, Los Angeles, California

2 cups whole unblanched
  almonds (about 10 ounces),
  divided
11 ounces milk chocolate,
  divided
2 sticks sweet butter
1 cup sugar
3 tablespoons cold water

Spread almonds in a pan and toast in a 350° oven for about 10 minutes, shaking pan occasionally. Cool. Grind chocolate fine in food processor—*do not overprocess*. Set aside. Chop almonds coarse in food processor; sprinkle 1 cup over bottom of a greased 15-in. x 10-in. x 1-in. jelly roll pan. Sprinkle 1 cup ground chocolate over nuts. Set aside. In a heavy saucepan, combine butter, sugar and water; cook over medium heat, stirring occasionally, until the mixture reaches 290° (soft-crack stage). *Very quickly* pour mixture over nuts and chocolate. Sprinkle remaining chocolate over; top with remaining nuts. Chill and break into pieces. **Yield:** about 2 pounds.

MACADAMIA NUT FUDGE

Vicki Fioranelli, Cleveland, Mississippi

4-1/2 cups sugar
1/2 cup sweet butter
1 can (12 or 13 ounces)
  evaporated milk
1 box (12 ounces) German
  sweet chocolate squares,
  chopped
1 package (12 ounces)
  semisweet chocolate chips
1 jar (7 ounces) marshmallow
  creme
1 teaspoon salt (omit if using
  salted nuts)
2 teaspoons vanilla extract
3 cups crushed macadamia
  nuts *or* toasted pecans,
  divided

Combine sugar, butter and milk in heavy pan; bring to a gentle boil. Cook for 5 minutes, stirring constantly. Remove from heat; add remaining ingredients except 1 cup nuts. Pour into two 9-in. square greased or waxed paper-lined pans; sprinkle remaining nuts over top and press in lightly. Chill until firm; cut into squares. **Yield:** about 5 pounds.

MOUNDS BALLS

Kathy Dorman, Snover, Michigan

1/2 pound sweet butter
1 pound confectioners' sugar
1 pound flaked coconut
1/2 can (7 ounces) *or* 1/2 cup
  sweetened condensed milk
1 cup chopped walnuts
1 teaspoon vanilla extract
CHOCOLATE COATING:
1 package (12 ounces)
  semisweet chocolate chips
4 ounces unsweetened
  chocolate squares
2-inch x 1-inch x 1/2-inch piece of
paraffin wax
Round wooden toothpicks
Styrofoam sheets

In mixing bowl, cream butter and sugar. Add coconut, milk, walnuts and vanilla; stir until blended. Chill until slightly firm; roll into walnut-size balls. Insert a toothpick in each ball. Place balls on cookie sheets; freeze. In double boiler over simmering water, melt chocolate chips, squares and paraffin. Keep warm over hot water. Using toothpicks as handles, dip frozen balls into chocolate mixture; stick picks upright into waxed paper-covered Styrofoam sheets. Chill until firm. Remove picks and package candy in individual paper liners. (May also be frozen.) **Yield:** about 7 dozen.

EASY MICROWAVE CARAMELS

Darleen Worm, Fond du Lac, Wisconsin

1 cup sweet butter
2-1/3 cups (1 pound) firmly packed
  brown sugar
1 cup light corn syrup
1 can (14 ounces) sweetened
  condensed milk
1/8 teaspoon salt
1 teaspoon vanilla extract
1/2 cup chopped walnuts,
  optional

In 2-qt. microwave-safe pitcher, combine butter, sugar, syrup, milk and salt. Microwave (MW) on high (100% power) 3 to 4 minutes, stirring once after about 2 minutes. When butter is melted, stir well. Attach *microwave* candy thermometer. MW on high about 14 minutes or until mixture reaches 245° (firm-ball stage). No stirring is needed. Remove from microwave; stir in vanilla and walnuts, if desired. Allow to stand for 10 minutes, stirring well several times. Pour into buttered 13-in. x 9-in. x 2-in. pan (11-in. x 7-in. x 1-1/2-in. pan yields thicker candy as shown in

photo). Refrigerate until cool. Invert pan. Carefully tap out whole block of candy; cut into squares. Wrap in waxed paper and store in refrigerator (can also freeze). **Yield:** about 2-3/4 pounds.

ORANGE SUGARED PECANS

Murri Mills, Brady, Texas

1 cup packed brown sugar
3 tablespoons evaporated milk
1 tablespoon butter
1 teaspoon freshly grated
  orange peel
2 cups pecan halves

In small heavy saucepan, combine sugar and milk. Cook over medium heat to 234° (soft-ball stage), stirring occasionally. Add butter and orange peel; stir to blend. Add pecan halves; stir until all are coated. Spread pecans on parchment paper or a greased cookie sheet. When the coating is firm, gently break pecans apart. Store in covered containers. **Yield:** 4 cups.

CHOCOLATE ALMOND TRUFFLES

Arla Railsback, New Richmond, Wisconsin

1/2 cup heavy whipping cream
3-1/2 tablespoons sweet butter
8 ounces semisweet chocolate
  chips
1/4 teaspoon almond flavoring *or*
  1/4 cup Amaretto liqueur
Finely ground toasted almonds,
  chocolate sprinkles, chopped
  shredded coconut, cocoa powder
  or confectioners' sugar for
  coating

In a medium saucepan, heat cream and butter over medium-high, stirring until butter melts and mixture comes just to a boil. Remove pan from heat; add chocolate and stir until completely melted. Stir in flavoring or liqueur. Cover, placing paper towels between lid and saucepan to absorb moisture, if desired. Chill at least 3 hours, stirring three to four times as mixture cools and thickens. Remove about 1-1/2 teaspoons at a time and roll into balls. Roll balls in choice of coating. Refrigerate until ready to serve. Store in refrigerator. **Yield:** about 3-1/2 dozen 1-inch balls.

> **COOL CASHEWS:** Store nuts in the refrigerator in airtight containers to keep them fresh for holiday eating and baking.

STUFFED DATES

Dorothy Pepper, Thermal, California

12 large dates, suitable for stuffing
1 package (3 ounces) cream cheese, softened
3 tablespoons orange marmalade
Walnut halves

Carefully cut dates in half; remove pits. Set aside. Combine cream cheese and marmalade until smooth. Toast walnut halves in a 350° oven for about 10 minutes; cool. Using small spoon, fill date halves with cream cheese mixture. Top each with a walnut half. Store, covered, in refrigerator. **Yield:** 12 stuffed dates.

MICROWAVE LECHE QUEMADA

Mildred Kneupper, New Braunfels, Texas

2 cups pecans (small or broken pieces)
1/2 cup sweet butter
2/3 cup packed brown sugar
1 can (14 ounces) sweetened condensed milk
1 teaspoon vanilla extract

Place pecans on large glass plate and microwave (MW) on high (100% power) for 8 minutes, stirring at 2-minute intervals. Set aside. In 8-cup measure, MW butter on high for 1 minute. Stir in brown sugar and milk until blended. MW on high for 7 minutes, stirring at 2-minute intervals. Beat with wooden spoon until stiff, about 5 minutes. Stir in vanilla and roasted pecans. Spread in lightly buttered 8-in. square glass dish; chill until firm. Cut into squares. **Yield:** 1-1/2 pounds.

TWO-TONE FUDGE

Lavonne Sullivan, Topeka, Kansas

2 cups packed brown sugar
1 cup sugar
1 cup evaporated milk
1/2 cup sweet butter
1 jar (7 ounces) marshmallow creme
1 teaspoon vanilla extract
1 package (6 ounces) butterscotch chips
1 cup coarsely chopped walnuts, *divided*
1 package (6 ounces) semisweet chocolate chips

In saucepan, combine sugars, milk and butter. Bring to full boil over moderate heat, stirring constantly. Boil for 10 minutes, stirring occasionally. Remove from heat. Add marshmallow creme and vanilla; stir until mixture is smooth. Remove 2 cups of hot mixture; add butterscotch chips and 1/2 cup walnuts. Stir until chips are melted and mixture is smooth. Pour evenly into a greased 9-in. square pan; place in freezer to chill while preparing second layer. To remaining hot mixture, add chocolate chips and remaining walnuts. Stir until chips are melted and mixture is smooth. Pour evenly over the butterscotch mixture in pan. Chill until firm. **Yield:** 2-1/2 pounds.

GARDEN GIFTS: Fill small plastic bags with homegrown dried herbs and tie with ribbon. Or, put flower seeds from your garden in small, pretty envelopes.

SPICED MIXED NUTS

Joanne Warner, Baldwin, Wisconsin

1 egg white, lightly beaten
1 teaspoon water
1 jar (8 ounces) dry roasted peanuts
1/2 cup unblanched whole almonds
1/2 cup walnut *or* pecan halves
3/4 cup sugar
1 tablespoon pumpkin pie spice

In a large bowl, combine egg white and water. Add nuts; toss to coat. Combine sugar and spice; sprinkle over the nuts and toss until well coated. Place nuts in a single layer on lightly greased baking sheet. Bake at 300° for 20-25 minutes. Immediately transfer the nuts to waxed paper; cool. Break up any large clusters. Store in a covered container. **Yield:** 6 cups.

CANDIED CITRUS PEELS

Mary Malinowski, Lee Center, New York

2 cups fresh orange, grapefruit *or* lemon peels (about 4 fruits)
Cold water
SYRUP:
1 cup sugar
1/2 cup water
Confectioners' sugar

CHOCOLATE COATING:
8 ounces semisweet chocolate chips
4 ounces unsweetened chocolate
2-inch x 1-inch x 1/2-inch piece of paraffin wax

Using a metal zester or similar tool, cut peels from fruits in 1/4-in.-wide strips 3 in. long. Place peels in heavy saucepan; cover with cold water. Bring slowly to boiling; reduce heat and simmer 10 minutes. Drain; repeat boiling process 3 to 5 times, draining well each time. (This cooks the peels and eliminates bitterness of membrane.) In a separate saucepan, combine sugar and water; cook until clear. Add peels; boil gently until all syrup is absorbed and peels are transparent. Roll peels in confectioners' sugar; place on cooling rack to dry. Combine chocolate coating ingredients in top of double boiler; melt together over simmering water until smooth. Dip half of each peel in chocolate; cool on rack sprayed with no-stick cooking spray. Store, covered, in refrigerator. **Yield:** about 3 cups.

ORANGE/CHOCOLATE SUGARPLUMS

Evelyn Skaggs, Nixa, Missouri

2 cups coarsely chopped pecans
2 cups coarsely chopped unblanched almonds
1 cup orange marmalade
1/2 cup flaked coconut
1 package (8 ounces) semisweet chocolate
1 egg, beaten
Confectioners' sugar

In a large bowl, mix pecans, almonds, marmalade and coconut. Set aside. In a small saucepan, melt chocolate at low temperature; remove from heat and cool 15 minutes. Beat egg into chocolate until mixture is smooth. Stir chocolate into nut mixture; chill 1 hour or until firm enough to handle. Shape into walnut-size balls. Roll in confectioners' sugar. Store, covered, in refrigerator. **Yield:** about 5 dozen.

QUICK & EASY CHRISTMAS CANDY

CANDY is dandy for holiday gift-giving...so when you're down to your "last-minute" list, look to these speedy sweets for a satisfying solution.

SNAPPY SWEETS like chocolaty pretzels and nutty brittle bits microwave in minutes!

WHITE CHOCOLATE PRETZELS

Jenny Riegsecker, Delta, Ohio

- 12 ounces white chocolate, chopped
- 1 package (6 ounces) semisweet chocolate chips
- 2 to 3 dozen whole twisted pretzels
- Finely chopped nuts, optional

Melt white chocolate in microwave or double boiler. With tongs, dip pretzels, one at a time, in chocolate. Let excess chocolate run off back into pan. Place dipped pretzels on waxed paper to cool; chill to harden slightly. Melt the semisweet chocolate; cool several minutes. Using a pastry bag with small round pastry tip (or a plastic bag with the tip snipped off or a large spoon), drizzle dark chocolate squiggles over coated pretzels. Immediately sprinkle with nuts, if desired. Chill.

MICROWAVE PEANUT BRITTLE

Sue Moore, Hartwell, Georgia

- 1 cup raw peanuts
- 1 cup sugar
- 1/2 cup white corn syrup
- 1/8 teaspoon salt
- 1 teaspoon butter
- 1 teaspoon vanilla extract
- 1 teaspoon baking soda

In a 1-1/2-qt. casserole, stir together peanuts, sugar, syrup and salt. Microwave (MW) on high (100% power) for 4 minutes; stir well and MW for 4 minutes more. Stir in the butter and vanilla. MW 2 minutes longer. Add baking soda and quickly stir until light and foamy. *Immediately* pour onto lightly greased cookie sheet, spreading out thin. Cool; break into small pieces. Store in an airtight container. **Yield:** about 1 pound.

DATE NUT BALLS

Myrtle McSwan, Indio, California

- 1 cup pitted dates
- 1 cup raisins
- 1/2 cup dried apricots
- 1/2 cup pitted prunes *or* figs
- Unsweetened orange juice to moisten
- Flaked coconut *or* chopped walnuts

In food grinder, grind together dates, raisins, apricots and prunes or figs. Combine with orange juice in 2-qt. mixing bowl. Roll into bite-size balls. Roll in coconut or nuts. Refrigerate, covered, until time to serve. **Yield:** about 2 dozen.

EASY SPICED NUTS

Coral Rhoda, Holland, Michigan

- 1 egg white
- 1 teaspoon cold water
- 1 pound (4 cups) pecan halves
- 1/2 cup sugar
- 1/4 teaspoon salt
- 1/2 teaspoon cinnamon

Beat egg white slightly; add water. Beat until frothy but not stiff. Pour over pecans in a large bowl; stir until nuts are coated. Mix sugar, salt and cinnamon. Sprinkle over nuts; mix well. Pour into a 13-in. x 9-in. x 2-in. buttered pan; bake at 250° for 1 hour. Stir once or twice while baking. **Yield:** about 6 cups.

CINNAMON CHEWS

Paula Johnson, Eaton, Colorado

- 1 pound marshmallows
- 1 package (9 ounces) red-hot cinnamon candies
- 3 tablespoons butter
- 1/2 teaspoon salt
- 2-1/2 cups crisp rice cereal
- Confectioners' sugar

Combine all ingredients except cereal and sugar and melt in top of a double boiler. When melted, add cereal, mixing quickly. Spread in buttered 8-in. square pan. Chill; cut in 1/2-in. squares. Dust with confectioners' sugar. Wrap individually in waxed paper.

BLUEBERRY CLUSTERS

June Pothier, Norristown, Pennsylvania

- 2 cups (11-1/2 ounces) milk chocolate chips
- 1/4 cup butter *or* margarine
- 2 cups fresh blueberries, washed and dried
- 1-1/2-inch paper candy liners

Over hot (not boiling) water, combine chips and butter. Stir until mixture is melted and smooth. Remove from heat. Place 1 teaspoon of melted chocolate in paper candy liner. Add 6 to 8 blueberries; top with 2 teaspoons chocolate, making sure the blueberries are well coated. Chill 20-30 minutes. Serve at room temperature for up to 1 hour; store in refrigerator.

QUICK TURTLES

Fern Lockwood, Daytona Beach, Florida

- 1-1/2 cups pecan halves
- 1 package (14 ounces) vanilla caramels
- 5 bars (1-1/2 ounces *each*) milk chocolate

Arrange pecan halves in clusters of 3 or 4, 2 in. apart on a greased baking sheet. Top each cluster with one caramel, slightly flattened. Bake at 300° for 7 minutes or until caramels soften. Remove to waxed paper. Flatten caramels with spatula; top each candy with a milk chocolate bar while still warm. Spread chocolate when melted. Refrigerate a few minutes until chocolate hardens. **Yield:** 4 dozen.

M-M-MERRY CHRISTMAS! Good giving can include jars of crab apple/basil jelly (below) among many homegrown holiday ideas.

CRAB APPLE/BASIL JELLY
3 pounds crab apples (slightly underripe)
1 sprig cinnamon *or* lemon basil (about 10 to 14 leaves)
2-1/2 to 3 cups sugar

Wash crab apples; remove the stems and blossom ends. Cover with water in a large stainless or ceramic pot; add washed sprig of cinnamon or lemon basil. Simmer until the apples are soft. Drain juice overnight through jelly bag or clean dish towel. Bring 4 cups of the drained juice (add water to make 4 cups if necessary) to a boil in a very large stainless or ceramic pot. Add sugar and boil to sheeting stage (when the drips sheet together off the side of a stainless spoon). Skim. Pour into sterile jelly jars. Skim again and seal with two thin layers of paraffin, making certain the second layer seals to glass edges. **Yield:** about 5 cups of bright red jelly.

'Pick' Perfect Presents!

By Cynthia Driscoll, Grand Rapids, Minnesota

PLANT SMILES on the faces of family and friends this year with gifts from your garden!

Even the simplest, easiest-to-grow fruits and vegetables are great for giving and especially appreciated by folks whose thumbs may not be as green as yours are. In fact, some presents require only the picking—a big bowl of bright, sweet-tart apples ...or a basket that's mounded high with green and yellow gourds...or a braid of golden onions.

What cook wouldn't welcome an old-fashioned onion braid? Hanging conveniently in a country kitchen, dried onions or shallots—with their warm, coppery colors—add a mellow and friendly feeling to any country decor. And the bulbs are always at the ready to be snipped as seasoning for stuffings and stews.

Other homegrown gifts you can gather necessitate only a little pre-planning.

In early autumn, while my family's busy harvesting the last of our garden produce, my mind's on another season. I contemplate Christmas as I put up dilled beans, spiced peaches, brandied crab apples, strawberry-rhubarb jam ("rhuberry", we call it), mint jelly, apple butter, seven varieties of pickles, canned or frozen pumpkin, clear plum jelly and—a big favorite—crab apple/basil jelly (see recipe at top right).

As I work, I make a mental gift list, checking off the special taste preferences of family and friends. Later, as I wrap my green and red rewards, I can't help but smile at the fruits of my labor. There won't be any need for me to hunt in a hurry through crowded stores at the last minute for the perfect present!

Garden garnishes make great gifts, too—a true feast for the eyes! Hone homemade wreaths from evergreen and pine boughs, accent with orange Chinese lanterns and adorn with red and green calico ribbons. Or give garlands of glistening cayenne peppers, dried and strung before the first frost.

Mix some sowing and sewing by stringing together popcorn and small highbush or wild cranberries for giveaway garlands—they'll add the perfect festive flair to any Christmas tree or bannister. Heap be-ribboned baskets or earthenware bowls with tiny ears of strawberry popcorn for a pretty present that can serve as a centerpiece and snack!

Bring back the sweet scents of summer with gifts of herbs in potpourris and sachets. Package dried, crushed herb seasonings in small jars with shaker tops, or twine your own blend of whole dried herbs into decorative cooking wreaths. Mull homegrown mint or lemon balm tea. Gather garden-grown basils, dill seed or weed and summer savory in pretty,

corked glass vials neatly tied with colorful ribbon.

For a fun flourish, fashion gifts from dried strawflowers. Every year I order a few new-to-me varieties from seed houses specializing in display flowers and grasses.

I've had especially good luck with Helichrysum. It's a vivid easy-to-dry strawflower which I combine with baby's breath and display in small ceramic or glass bottles. I usually keep a tray of herb and dried flower packages near my front door to treat drop-in visitors during the holidays.

Don't forget your many feathered friends when you make out a garden-gift list! Serve them up a sumptuous suet of sunflower seeds...colorful corn varieties...red, white and variegated beans, nuts, peas and even beet seeds.

Seed ornaments can add interest to Christmas trees, too. And kids love to glue seeds onto Styrofoam shapes or hand-drawn pictures to give to Grandma or Grandpa.

The possibilities are plentiful... plus there are no parking problems when you "shop" in your own backyard garden! So consider homegrown goodness for this Christmas. You'll find few gifts as gratifying to give—or more gratefully received!

The Great Gift of Grandkids

"KEEP THIS UNDER YOUR HAT!" Thaddeus Dammon seems to be saying to cousin Helena Hagedorn. "All he really wanted was a chance to wear her Christmas cap," Grandma Mavis Dittmer of Washington, Kansas recalls.

"GOD'S GREATEST GIFT" is how DeLoris Kusler of Lodi, California describes her grandchildren. "We taught them the Christmas story as they posed for this picture we used to send holiday greetings," she notes.

TICKLISH WHISKERS touched off Amber Marie York's giggles, laughs Great-Grandmother Thelma Jacks of Nokomis, Florida. Amber soon found what a bowlful of jelly feels like when Santa started "ho-ho-hoing", too!

WHAT CHILD IS THIS? Little Jessica Haaser peeks into Great-Grandmother Rose Kiene's glowing Nativity scene—made from a tree root—during a Christmas visit to Rudy, Arkansas. Rose treasures both dearly!

BAAA...HUMBUG! Young Michael tries to get his new goat, "Gotcha", to catch the Christmas spirit, writes Grandmother Harriett Glaze of Redding, California. "Those two are the best of friends," she adds.

PICK OF THE LITTER greets Katie Christensen on the fringe of her first-Christmas blanket. "The piglet was just 1 day old when it came to make friends," says Grandma Jan of West Bend, Iowa about the two babies.

PIG HEADED her grandsons, Adam (right) and Brett, in right direction..."after plenty of persuading," reports Dorothy Pedersen of Ledyard, Iowa. "Getting that pig to hold still and our little farmers to smile was fun!"

Christmas
POETRY CORNER

THE GIFTS WE'RE GIVEN

If every gift was taken from
Beneath the Christmas tree,
And everything was gone except
The love of family…

Then we would still have everything
That makes the season real,
For Christmas joy is in the way
We make each other feel.

Just as long as love was there
Along with faith so sweet,
We'd still have a Christmas that
Was perfectly complete.

**Hilda Sanderson
Calhoun, Louisiana**

Dennis Barnes

WORTH PRESERVING!

When the pantry is full it means only one thing—
The end of the garden we planted in spring.
There's catsup and peppers and pickles galore,
And carrots, tomatoes and peas and much more.

When the pantry is full it means winter is near;
The snow and the sleet will be falling soon here…
The leaves all have floated fall colors around;
Now the last of the chestnuts has thumped to the ground.

When the pantry is full the feeling is good—
Now is the time to be gathering wood,
For winter will bring a warmth and a glow
While we sit snug and cozy and gaze at the snow.

When the pantry is full you know love's in the heart,
For lots of your time went into each part—
To pick and to clean, to wash and to can,
All labors of love for your family and man.

When the pantry is full you feel good inside,
As you look on your jars with a feeling of pride.
There they all stand like a real work of art,
All pretty as pictures…now don't you feel smart?

Through all of the "putting up" you've worked like a mule,
But don't you feel good when the pantry is full?

Betty Sutter, Shingletown, California

Bob Taylor

H. Armstrong Roberts

SNOW SOUND

How still, how still
The snowflakes all
As from the sky
They gently fall.
They sweep the step
And tip the tree;
Land on the lawn
So silently.
A million fall
With calm and poise,
And not one makes
A bit of noise.
They lace the lake
And hide the hill,
Soundlessly,
So still,
So still.

**O.J. Robertson
Russell Springs,
Kentucky**

My Greatest Christmas Gift Ever!

By Jane K. Mitchell, Underhill, Vermont

I was only 6 then, but I remember it as vividly as though it happened yesterday. As soon as we finished dinner that Christmas Eve, my older brother went to the attic for the box that held our Christmas stockings.

There were eight stockings, one for each member of the family, and our initials were woven in red thread on the white cuff at the top. We always hung them in order, from oldest to youngest, starting at the left-hand side of the mantel and working to the right. First my father, then my mother, followed by my brother and us five girls.

Each of us took our own stocking from the box, shaking it to see if just maybe we had overlooked a coin or a candy before we put it away last year. But on that Christmas Eve the year I was 6, there was one stocking left in the box, and I didn't want to look at it. My mother picked it up and smoothed the wrinkles with her hand, stroking it as if it were a cat lying across her legs.

"The baby can use Daddy's stocking this year," she said. "After all, they have the same initials."

"But what if Santa thinks...?" I pleaded.

"Don't worry," my mother assured me. "Santa knows."

So we hung the eight stockings, this time with my mother's stocking first in line and my father's stocking —which now belonged to the baby —at the tail of the line.

I was very confused that Christmas. Some of the kids in first grade with me said there was no such thing as Santa Claus, that mothers and fathers filled the stockings and put presents under the tree. If they were right, it meant that we might not have any Christmas this year, because my father had just died.

There was a lot of sadness in our house, and my mother was doing her best to disguise it. But if there was a Santa, he might not know about my father and then he'd fill the baby's stocking with flashlight batteries and new razor blades and the hard, butter rum candies my father had liked to suck on. I wished we could just skip Christmas that year.

After the stockings were hung we were allowed to bring our presents to each other from their hiding places. If we put them out any earlier than Christmas Eve, there had always been too much peeking and shaking and poking of the presents.

There were more presents for my mother than usual that year, because we had all made something for our father, not knowing he was going to die before Christmas. Everything except the tie rack my sister had made could be used by a lady, so my mother got double presents.

We set out cookies and milk for Santa as usual. If the kids at school were right, my father, not Santa, had been the one to eat the cookies and drink the milk. But my father was gone, and my mother didn't like milk.

I also insisted we leave Fig Newtons with the milk, because I knew my mother hated them. If the milk and cookies were still there in the morning, I would know the truth.

Two of my sisters and I shared a bedroom. A radio the size of a jukebox stood between the beds, and the year before we had been allowed to listen to *A Christmas Carol* as we lay in the dark.

I had been frightened by the ghost of Christmas Past last year, and my father had sat and listened with us and told us what a lovely story it was.

No one suggested we listen this year. So it was very quiet lying there in the dark, quiet enough to hear footsteps on the roof, if you believed in that sort of thing. But all I could hear was the silence downstairs.

It was barely light when I awoke Christmas morning. The yard light outside my window was still on, and from where I lay I could see huge flakes of snow floating into the yellow pool of light.

I stayed in bed, watching the lazy flakes drifting down, wishing that

🍃•🍃

"The baby can use Daddy's stocking this year."

everyone in the house would just sleep through Christmas. That way when we woke up, everything might be fine again.

My younger sister was next to wake up, and there was no stopping her. I couldn't tell her that the stockings might not have anything in them this year, but at least I could go with her. She first woke up everyone else, and we all went to my mother's room. I wanted to leave Mother out of this, but she was up and ready to go downstairs with us.

My brother stopped at the head of the stairs and said, "There's something down there!" In the dim light that came through the frosted glass in the front door we could see a large shape slumped against the wall.

"What is it?" he asked my mother, and we all waited for her answer.

"I don't know," she said slowly, squinting through the gloom. "I really don't know!"

We all moved cautiously down the stairs, peering over each other's shoulders. "It's a stocking," my brother finally said, "a huge stocking!"

Propped up against the doors leading into the living room was an enormous stocking, taller than me and so big that I could not reach my arms around it. It was filled with presents, some for each child and for my mother as well.

I looked at my mother. Her eyes

were filled with tears and she was shaking her head slowly back and forth. She kept saying, "But who could have done this?" as though one of us might know.

Someone had come quietly in the night and left this stocking, and she really had no idea who that someone was. I learned much later that it was many years before she had a clue.

But I knew that day. Maybe my parents had played Santa before, but this year, when we really needed him, Santa had come. He had filled our stockings and left gifts under the tree and had eaten his snack, too.

I'm sure we had a lovely day, but I don't remember it. My memory of that Christmas stops at the bottom of the stairs, seeing that huge stocking.

Many years later—when I was grown and had a 6-year-old of my own—I asked my mother about that Christmas long ago. Her face softened at the memory. She really had known nothing about the stocking that morning long ago, and it was a number of years before she learned that our neighbors had made the stocking, bought and wrapped the gifts and sneaked it into our house on Christmas Eve.

I was touched by the kindness of those good country people. How much they gave us that day I'm sure they never knew. Not only did they give their gift of toys, but they gave me back my belief in Santa Claus.

Their gift has grown more dear to me with time. I see it now as the special gift of good friends and kind neighbors—the gift of love.

'Tis the Season to Be Frantic

By Jane Goodsell
Greensburg, Indiana

How do I know it's Christmastime?
Let me count the ways:
The children are hysterical,
And I am in a daze.
The house looks like a parrot cage:
We're ankle-deep in litter—
Ribbon, paper, seals and tags,
Styrofoam and glitter.
Packages and Christmas cards
Lie scattered on the stairs.
Holly berries squish beneath
The cushions of the chairs.
The children, with fanatic zeal,
Glue miles of paper chains,
While taking turns at licking
Each other's candy canes.
Whatever are they up to now?
They're making cookie dough.
They roll it on the kitchen floor
While flour drifts like snow.

How do I know it's Christmastime?
Because I lie in bed,
Wide-awake as shopping lists
Dance through my whirling head.
What should I send to Auntie Maud?
A purse? A book? Cologne?
A gadget for her phone?
And what about the Burtons' child?
We'd better send a toy.
The trouble is, I can't recall
If it's a girl or boy.
Does Uncle Henry smoke cigars?
How old's the Bensons' child?
Are Bill and Mary Scott divorced,
Or are they reconciled?
I wish I knew how many kids
The Matthews have produced.
What size does Cousin May wear now?
(I hear that she's reduced.)

How do I know it's Christmastime?
Because I'm in a tizzy.
I've got so many things to do
I'm absolutely dizzy.
I must address the Christmas cards.
Now where—oh, dear! Oh, dear!
I wonder where on earth I put
That list I made last year.
I promised I'd make cookies for
The yearly church bazaar.
I've got to find the tree lights,
And I can't think where they are.

It's obvious it's Christmastime.
The windowpanes are frosted.
The halls are decked with holly boughs,
And I am plumb exhausted.
And yet, despite the stress and strain
Involved in Christmas cheer,
I'll tell you something frankly:
It's my favorite time of year.

Holiday Barn Brings Year-Round Cheer

By Pat Vojtech
Centreville, Maryland

"I *LOVE* Christmas," confesses Mary Scheeler. And you don't have to look any farther than her farm family's old barn for the stuffed-to-the-rafters evidence!

Where cows and horses once were sheltered, tens of thousands of ornaments now overflow in her unique Christmas store. They provide shoppers a spirited immersion in the season.

Over almost every foot of the first floor is some sparkling morsel of a country Christmas—from reindeer right down to the *complete* collection of Dickens' village. One corner offers up an array of nutcrackers and smokers so impressive it may be the best outside New York City.

"Christmas has *always* been important to me," Mary points out. And she likes nothing better than helping to introduce its wonders to others. "I especially like to watch the children who come along with their parents to the shop. When they spot my 3-foot-tall Santa doll, do their little eyes get big!"

Since the Scheelers' Eastern shore location supplies Mary with a sizable number of city visitors, their young vistas also often widen. Walking from car to the Christmas barn, boys and girls more accustomed to concrete than to combines just might spot Mike Scheeler and his father, Charles, active in the fields. This is a *work-*

🎄

"Christmas lets us see all over again how special people are."

MARY SCHEELER fashions holiday wreaths (above) and an amazing array of ornaments and other collectibles (top) to fill her barn with Christmas spirit.

ing farm. And even in Mary's barn, reminders remain.

Shoppers—on their way to get a closer look at the holiday goodies that hang from hefty, hand-hewn chestnut timbers—still step over the beams that frame each stall. A harness rack holds candle rings. Rising up to an antique-filled hayloft is a wooden ladder.

"It's all a part of the charm of coming here," she explains.

"Charm" or not, Mary admits the barn wasn't her initial choice when Mike suggested she move her Christmas shop there. "That was in 1976. I'd already outgrown our living room and even an extra room we'd added on.

"But the *barn*?" she says of the huge dairy building that dates back to the 1830's. "It was so cold and damp—and too big! I didn't think I would *ever* fill it up."

A century and a half of animal habitation had left behind another potential problem. The old wood-and-peg barn was so dirty a bucket and a brush couldn't even make a dent. Luckily, Mike was a member of the local volunteer fire company, which loaned him a highly effective high-powered hose!

Now warm and inviting—and as clean as a choirboy on Christmas—the barn brims with the holidays…and the spirit of a country woman who appreciates them.

"I'm not doing all this to make money as much as to meet people," Mary reflects. "I look forward to seeing people come in and enjoy themselves, even if they don't buy a single thing.

"I believe Christmas comes to let us see all over again how special people are. And if I see a person only once, but I see that person happy because of something I've done, I couldn't feel better!"

Mary's store hours at Greenfield Farm near Ceciltown, Maryland are 10 a.m.-5 p.m. Wednesdays, Fridays and Saturdays and noon-5 p.m. Sundays. On other days, she says, "Call first!" (1-301/275-2267) and adds that she's not open "when there's ice in the driveway!" Mary stocks Christmas merchandise all year long, as well as antiques, dollhouses, miniatures and quilts.

HARK! THE HERALD ANGELS SING

Charles Wesley

Mendelssohn

Gift of Faith Still Shines

THE HOLIDAYS have been even brighter around Dunlap, Iowa since Agnes Dunham discovered just how powerful candles can be.

"I was making Christmas candles years ago," Agnes, now a retired farm wife, recalls. "And as I worked, I saw that I could mold the wax into any shape I wanted."

Playfully, she formed a face that resembled that of her husband, Don, then put a hat atop it for him to chuckle over.

But as Agnes looked at her humorous handiwork, she was struck with a second thought. And that inspiration has grown into one of the most unique celebrations of Christmas in the country.

Beginning in 1951, when Agnes molded eight figures, visitors have been drawn to Dunlap from miles away to view the result —a life-size wax Nativity scene.

"Our little town has always had some friendly competition for the best front-yard Christmas display," Agnes says. "I started with Mary, Joseph, Baby Jesus, a lamb,

"Every time I see the Nativity, I feel again the true meaning of Christmas."

a shepherd boy, a burro and two chickens. Don set up a small stable."

The next year, Agnes added a wise man, a camel, an angel and a cow. And the year after that, she finished two more wise men and camels, a shepherd and another lamb.

Each one was an undertaking.

To achieve lifelike human heads, Agnes stuffed nylon stockings, covered them with tinfoil and then applied wax...with a tablespoon.

Animals were no easier. She and her sister, Evelyn Thompson, split and melted thousands of crayons to obtain accurate colors. Meanwhile, as the display spread, Don and his friends constructed a new home for it—a 50-ft. barn.

Thanks to continuing community-supported restoration, Agnes' wax work has thrilled thousands over the years. That thrills its creator.

"Many evenings, after the crowds were gone," Agnes admits, "I'd go out myself to look at the scene. I no longer live on the farm, but I

LIGHTING THE SKY in western Iowa each December is an inspiring life-size wax Nativity scene that Agnes Dunham (at top) crafted from melted candles.

still try to get there once a year.

"Every time I see the Nativity, I feel again the true meaning of Christmas."

To see the Dunlap Nativity Scene, go west half a mile from town on Hwy. 37 to F-51, then north a quarter mile. It can be viewed each December from 5 to 10 p.m. Monday-Saturday and noon to 10 p.m. Sunday.

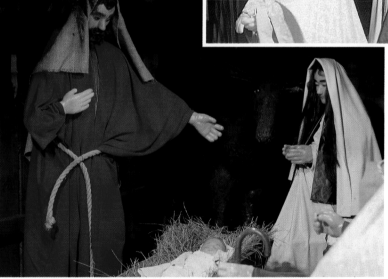

WE HAVE SEEN HIS STAR IN THE EAST

Laden with Gifts of Love

THE COUNTRYSIDE is an ideal setting to spread peace and goodwill to others, as evidenced by this gift-bearing boat that's headed across an Atlantic Ocean inlet for a nearby family's Christmas celebration in Rhode Island.

What better way to warm the hearts of friends and loved ones than with gifts lovingly created by hand? On the following pages, you'll find a variety of country crafts to make, ranging from crocheted snowflake ornaments to quilted holiday cards. To ensure that you can make gifts for everyone of your Christmas list, we chose craft projects that can be made economically and quickly!

YESTERDAY A CARD —TODAY A FAN!

WOULDN'T you like to make use of all the beautiful Christmas cards you receive? Now you can continue to enjoy them by creating charming Victorian fans.

These fans make a lovely table decoration or tree ornament. Or give them as a special gift—everyone will enjoy receiving a "touch of yesterday". Begin with the card selection and let your imagination do the rest.

CHRISTMAS CARD FANS

Materials needed: Christmas cards in all colors and finishes; scraps of lace, braid, ribbon and other trim; tacky glue; scissors; stapler; gold cord (optional).

Directions: Select cards approximately 7 x 5 inches in size. Since most fans are made from the front of the card, cut the card in half at the foldline. (Note: A card with a gold or silver back makes an elegant fan!)

Fold each card in "accordion" pleats, beginning and ending with the first and last pleat facing the back of the fan. After pleating, staple the folds together at one end to make a handle.

Glue lace or other trim to top edge of fan to enhance the color and design. (Tip: Spread glue on fan and allow it to become very tacky before applying trim.) Dry overnight.

Make a generous ribbon bow and glue to the handle. If you wish, glue small silk flowers or a holiday pick to the handle. To use the fan as a tree ornament, glue or sew a gold cord handle to the top of the fan.

Place a fan on each plate at your holiday dinner for a creative table decoration and thoughtful take-home remembrance. ✱

SACHETS MAKE SCENTS

AUNTIE, Grandma or Mom would love this basket filled with tiny sachets. They're easy to make—with 1-3/4-inch lace-edged ribbon—and will add welcome whiffs of fragrance to any room.

COUNTRY SACHETS IN BASKET

Materials needed: FOR SACHETS: Fragrant oil or perfume; 1-1/2 yards of 1-3/4-inch-wide lace-edged muslin ribbon; polyester stuffing; 12 small rosebud appliques; glue gun or craft glue. FOR BASKET: Round basket with about 3-1/2-inch diameter; 12-inch square of fabric; 3- x 28-inch strip of quilt batting; 1 yard of 1/2-inch-wide Cluny lace; 2/3 yard of 1/4-inch-wide satin ribbon; pinking shears; standard sewing supplies.

Directions:
SACHETS: For each sachet, cut a 4-1/2-inch length of lace-edged muslin ribbon. Fold under a 1/4-inch hem at top and glue. Fold bottom up 1-1/2 inches and glue lace edges together, forming a small pocket.

Put a drop of oil or perfume on a small piece of polyester stuffing and insert in pocket. Fold top flap down and glue in place to seal pocket. Glue a small applique to front of sachet.
BASKET: With top edge of batting strip about 1/2 inch below basket rim, wrap batting several times around basket to plump it up. Secure batting with glue. Measure outside of basket, from top of rim around bottom of basket to top of rim on other side. Add 1 inch to this measurement. Use pinking shears to cut a circle of fabric with this diameter. Stitch Cluny lace to wrong side of fabric circle so pinked edge of fabric overlaps bottom edge of lace by 1/4 inch. Pinked fabric edge will show on outside of basket.

Machine-baste a double row of stitches just below the lace. Pull the basting threads slightly to gather fabric. Place basket in center of fabric and pull threads firmly, arranging gathers evenly around the basket. When fabric fits snug around basket, knot thread ends securely.

Tie satin ribbon around basket just below rim and fill basket with sachets. ✱

Gift for Him
GLAD TIE-DINGS

IT'S OFTEN not easy to come up with just the right gift for men at Christmas—so here's a new twist on an age-old gift…the classic tie! This one uses a purchased pattern and attractive cross-stitch designs.

CROSS-STITCHED TIES

Materials needed: Charts; purchased tie pattern (omit interfacing requirements); 3/4 yard red 14-count Aida cloth or Fiddler's cloth (see note below); DMC six-strand embroidery floss in colors listed on color keys; size 24 tapestry needle; standard sewing supplies.

Note: Two or three ties can be made from 3/4 yard of fabric. If only one tie is being made, the same amount of fabric must be purchased because of pattern layout.

Directions: Following instructions on pattern, lay out and cut each tie. Make sure that both ends of each pattern piece are placed along vertical grain of Aida cloth. Use grain of fabric as your stitching guide. Sew up tie except for the center back seam.

Separate six-strand floss and use two strands to cross-stitch each design according to chart. To stitch, hold tie on diagonal as shown in Fig. 1, this will make it possible to stitch on straight of grain as you normally would.

Use arrows on chart as an aid to center design. Design can be placed anywhere within the bottom 8 inches of tie. Position design according to your own personal preference.

When stitching is complete, neatly hand-sew center back seam with matching thread. ✷

FIG 1
Dot indicates center of tie

Hold tie at this angle while stitching

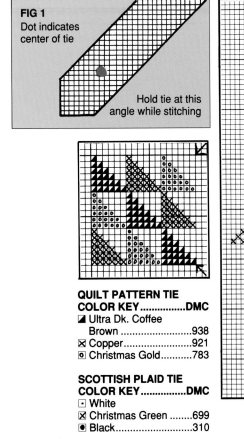

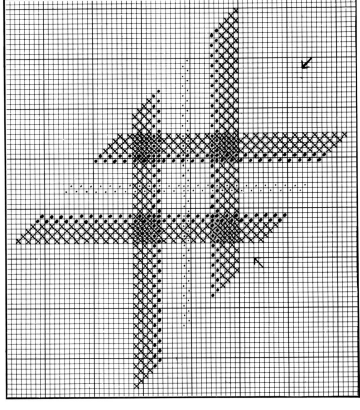

**QUILT PATTERN TIE
COLOR KEY...............DMC**
◪ Ultra Dk. Coffee
   Brown 938
⊠ Copper.......................921
◉ Christmas Gold...........783

**SCOTTISH PLAID TIE
COLOR KEY...............DMC**
⊡ White
⊠ Christmas Green 699
◉ Black...........................310

Gift for Her
A VESTED INTEREST

THIS bright red sweater vest will add zest to a favorite woman's winter wardrobe. And the quick-to-knit pattern comes in handy during the hustle-and-bustle holidays!

KNIT HOLIDAY VEST

Materials needed: Nos. 10 and 13 knitting needles; 4 skeins (125 yd/3 oz) 100% acrylic bulky-weight red yarn; darning needle.

Directions: Using No. 10 needles, cast on 55 sts. Begin with ribbing:
Row 1: * K 1, P 1, repeat from * across, ending with K 1.
Row 2: * P 1, K 1, repeat from * across, ending with P 1.
   Repeat rows 1 and 2 until ribbing measures 1 inch, ending with a row 2.
   Switch to No. 13 needles and body pattern:
Row 1: K 2, P 1, * (K 4, P 1, K 3, P 1) repeat from * 4 more times, end with K 4, P 1, K 2.
Row 2: Work stitches as they appear.
   Repeat these two rows until vest front is desired length, ending with a row 2.
   Switch to No. 10 needles and work ribbing for 1 inch, then bind off. Leave a long yarn tail for sewing up seams later.
   Make back of vest in exactly the same manner, following above procedure from casting on to binding off.
   Using darning needle and yarn tails, sew front and back of vest together 3 inches at each shoulder, leaving opening in center for neck. Secure yarn ends.
   Sew side seams, stitching about 6 to 8 inches up from bottom, leaving remaining areas open for armholes. Secure yarn ends.✳

Gift for Party Goers
FESTIVE FAVORS

THESE little bags are the perfect table favors for a festive holiday get-together—and a great project for young and old alike! Simply get out your odds and ends of paper, wrap up the styles and colors you want and fill them with mints and nuts. Then get ready for the rave reviews!

MINIATURE SHOPPING BAGS

Materials needed: Scraps of pretty paper; transparent tape; 6 inches of curling ribbon for each bag; scissors; pinking shears; 3-1/2- x 1-1/2- x 1-inch wooden block or similar-sized sturdy article.

Directions:

PAPER BAG: Cut a 6- x 3-1/2-inch rectangle from paper. Trim one 6-inch edge with pinking shears. This will be top edge of bag. Wrap paper around wooden block, extending the unpinked long edge beyond the block by 3/4 inch. Tape lengthwise seam.
   To close bottom of bag, fold in narrow sides first and then the other two sides, just as if you're wrapping a package. Crease all edges to make sharp straight edges and square corners. Tape bottom seam. Remove bag from the block and carefully fold sides and bottom "grocery bag style" as shown in photo. Fill as desired.

TOTE BAG: Cut a 6- x 7-inch rectangle from paper. Fold paper in half (wrong sides together) to make a 6- x 3-1/2-inch sheet. Wrap paper around wooden block, this time using the folded edge as the top of the bag.
   Crease and finish bag as above. Cut two 3-inch lengths of curling ribbon and tape ends inside top edge of bag to form handles. Fill as desired.✳

KID STUFF-ERS: You'll inspire big smiles (with little expense) when you fill children's stockings with fun items, such as lollipops dressed up with yarn hair, felt features and a bright fabric tie or lace collar.
   ● Glue pictures from an out-of-date calendar onto stiff cardboard and then cut it into pieces for a puzzle.
   ● Fashion ribbon, beads, barrettes, combs and small artificial flowers into pretty hair ornaments.
   ● Cover a small box with wrapping paper and fill with jelly beans or a favorite treat.

ALL DOLLED UP FOR CHRISTMAS

WRAP ONE of these cuddly critters with a bright bow and you'll have a huggable gift that's just right for a doll-loving child or crafter. (We liked them so much that we featured them on the cover of this book!) The cute crocheted bear turns a traditional technique into something warm and playful, and the simple kitty sock doll allows you to stitch up a variety of outfits if you wish. (The Velcro fasteners on the kitty's clothes are great for tiny fingers!)

CROCHETED BEAR

Materials needed: Reynolds LOPI, a 100% wool, bulky weight yarn in 100 gr/110 yd skeins (see shopping information below)—one skein each medium brown, burgundy and red; size G crochet hook; polyester stuffing; scrap of black felt; standard sewing supplies.

Finished size: Bear measures about 18 inches tall.

Shopping information: To find out where you may purchase LOPI yarn in your area, send a large self-addressed stamped envelope with your request to: Reynolds Yarns Inc., Dept. CH., PO Box 1176, 15 Oser Ave., Hauppauge NY 11788.

Gauge: 3 sc = 1 inch when worked in rounds with size G hook.

Directions: Bear parts are worked in continuous rounds with sc stitches. Work sc in both loops of sc in round below.

Snout: With brown, ch 4, join, and work 8 sc into circle. Work 2 sc in each sc until there are 18 sc. Work 5 rounds even.

Head: Next round, work 2 sc in each sc below (36 sc), work 2 rounds even, next round dec evenly to 30 sts, work 1 round even. Dec to 24 sts, work 1 round even. Dec to 18 sts, 1 round even. Dec to 14 sts, 1 round even. Firmly stuff head and sew hole in back of head closed.

Body: With burgundy, follow Fig. 1 and pick up 18 sc in circle at bottom of head. Next round, work 2 sc in each sc below. Work 1 round even. Work [2 rounds red, 3 rounds burgundy] two times. Work 1 very loose round of slip stitches in front loops of sc of previous round. Change to brown and work three rounds even. Stuff body.

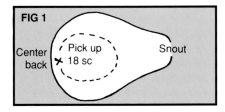

FIG 1

Center back — Pick up 18 sc — Snout

Leg: Working from center back to center front and continuing with brown, follow Fig. 2 and pick up 18 sc. Continue in rounds over these 18 sc and do 13 rounds even. Stuff leg. Next round dec to 9 sc (work sc 2 tog all around), then work 1 round even. Next round inc to 18 sts and work 3 rounds even. Next work [1 sc, sc 2 tog] around until 6 sc remain. Stuff foot and close up hole. Tack a small stitch through top of leg at hip. Work other leg in same manner.

FIG 2

Tack here

Stuffing

18 sc

Ear: Using brown and referring to Fig. 3, work 6 sc along surface of head. Work back and forth in sc rows, decreasing 1 sc at beginning of next two rows. End off. Attach yarn at base of ear and evenly sc around ear, causing the ear to cup slightly. Work other ear in same manner.

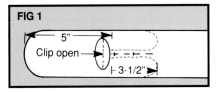

FIG 3   sc around

6 sc

Neckline: Attach burgundy at center back of neck. Work 1 slip stitch into every stitch around neck. End off.

Arm: With burgundy and referring to Fig. 4, pick up 14 sc and work 12 rounds even. Change to red and work 2 rounds even. Then slip-stitch around bottom round as you did for "hem edge" of sweater. Change to brown and work 2 rounds even. Next, work [1 sc, sc 2 tog] around until 6 sc remain. Stuff hand and close up hole. Work other arm in same manner.

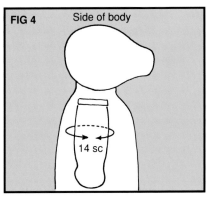

FIG 4   Side of body

14 sc

Facial features: Cut three small felt circles and sew to head with black sewing thread. Using white sewing thread, take a small stitch in each eye for highlighting. ✳

KITTY SOCK DOLL

Materials needed: Patterns; tracing or pattern paper; pencil; one pair toddler's socks, size 5 to 7-1/2; 12 inches of red bias binding; 1/4-inch piece of 1/2-inch-wide white Velcro; 1 yard tan yarn; 19 inches of 1/4-inch-wide white elastic; 25- x 4-inch piece white patterned fabric; 8- x 10-inch piece blue calico; 4- x 8-inch piece plaid fabric; scraps of red, tan and pink felt; black and magenta embroidery floss; a small amount of polyester stuffing; Aleene's tacky glue; standard sewing supplies.

Finished size: Kitty stands about 8-1/2 inches tall.

Directions: Trace all patterns to tracing paper and copy all notes and markings. Cut out all patterns. Sew pieces with right sides together and 1/4-inch seam allowances unless noted otherwise. Press seams open as you go.

Turn socks wrong side out and lay flat with heel facing up. Refer to Fig. 1 for following steps: On one sock, mark the point where heel begins (about 5 inches from toe) and mark point 3-1/2 inches above heel. With pins, mark a leg separation in the sock center between the two marks. It should be a narrow upside down "U" shape. Stitch legs. Trim away most of the seam allowances around legs.

FIG 1

5"

Clip open →

3-1/2"

Clip heel open and turn body right side out. Fill with polyester stuffing and neatly hand-sew opening closed. This side will be the doll's front. Tie a 6-inch piece of yarn around sock, about 2-1/2 inches from toe, to form neck. Cut six 5-inch lengths of yarn and knot together at one end. Braid yarn and knot other end. Sew to body for tail, about 1 inch above beginning of legs.

On foot of second sock, mark two 4-inch arms in same manner as you marked legs. Stitch arms and trim around edges. Turn arms right side out and fill with polyester stuffing. Turn in raw edges at openings and neatly hand-sew closed. Sew arm to each side of doll, directly below neck.

Cut two ears from tan felt and two inner ears from pink felt. Glue inner ears to ears, having straight edges even. When dry, sew ears to back of doll's head. Referring to Fig. 2 and color photo, embroider features onto face. Using three strands of magenta floss, backstitch mouth lines. With three strands black, satin-stitch nose and eyes. Make tiny black stitches for lashes and brows. Cut two pink felt cheeks and hand-sew to face with matching pink thread.

FIG 2

Using patterns, cut out dress, apron and pantaloons pieces. Hem sides and bottom of apron piece. Gather unhemmed apron edge to fit lower edge of one bodice piece between marks on pattern and pin and baste in place. Gather top edges of skirt pieces and pin and sew to lower edge of each bodice piece (one will have apron in between). Cut heart from red felt and topstitch to dress front with top half of heart on bodice and lower half of heart on apron. Sew bodices together at shoulders. ♂

Slightly gather sleeve tops and pin and sew into arm openings. Narrow-hem bottom sleeve edges and the bottom pantaloons edges. Cut four 3-1/4-inch lengths of elastic. Stretch each to fit on wrong side of sleeves and pantaloons, next to hems. Stitch in place while stretching elastic.

Cut center back of dress from neck edge to 1-3/4 inches below neck edge. Bind opening and neck edge with red bias binding. Sew Velcro closure to top of opening. Sew dress sides together, from sleeve hems to skirt bottom. Hem dress.

Sew center front seam of pantaloons. Zigzag waist edge and turn under 3/8 inch. Cut 6-inch piece of elastic and sew to inside waist, stretching it as you sew. Sew center back seam. Sew inner leg seams continuously from one hem to other hem. ✳

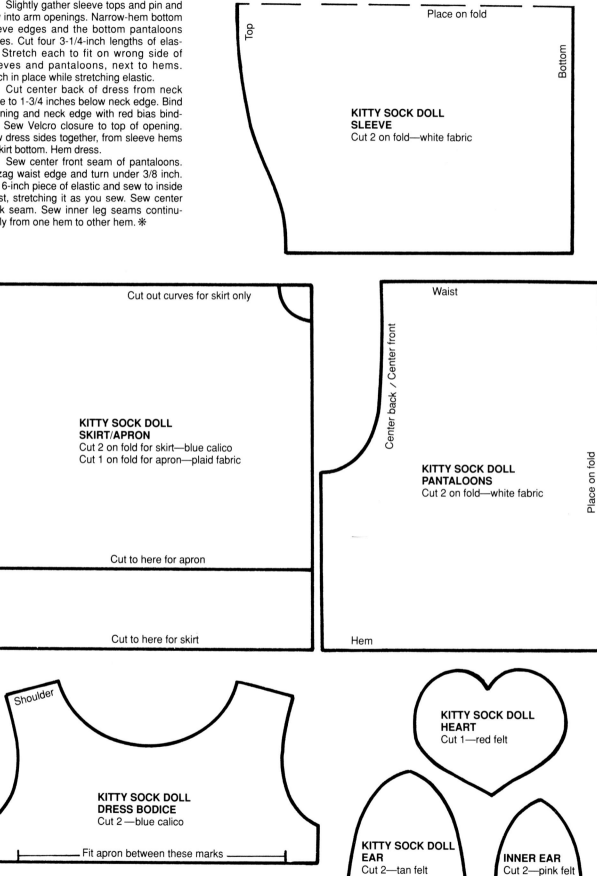

Place on fold

Top

Bottom

**KITTY SOCK DOLL
SLEEVE**
Cut 2 on fold—white fabric

Cut out curves for skirt only

Place on fold

**KITTY SOCK DOLL
SKIRT/APRON**
Cut 2 on fold for skirt—blue calico
Cut 1 on fold for apron—plaid fabric

Cut to here for apron

Cut to here for skirt

Waist

Center back / Center front

**KITTY SOCK DOLL
PANTALOONS**
Cut 2 on fold—white fabric

Place on fold

Hem

Shoulder

**KITTY SOCK DOLL
DRESS BODICE**
Cut 2—blue calico

Fit apron between these marks

**KITTY SOCK DOLL
HEART**
Cut 1—red felt

**KITTY SOCK DOLL
EAR**
Cut 2—tan felt

INNER EAR
Cut 2—pink felt

SEASON'S GREETINGS

HANDMADE CARDS are always well-received by friends and loved ones. These quilted cards use tried-and-true holly and star designs and let you make your message a personal one.

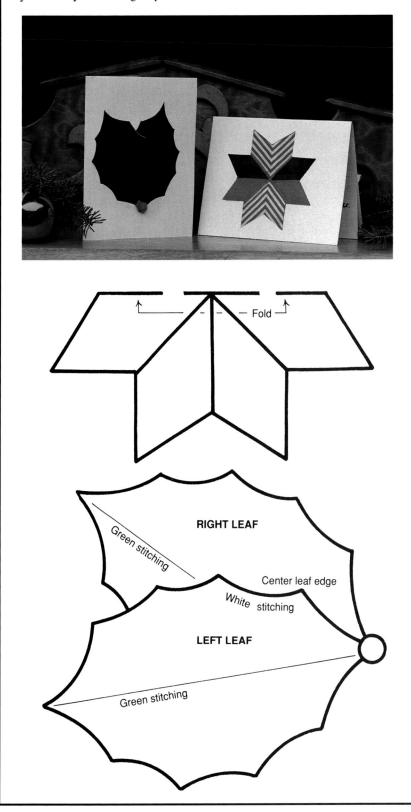

RIGHT LEAF

Green stitching

Center leaf edge

White stitching

LEFT LEAF

Green stitching

Fold

QUILTED HOLIDAY CARDS

Materials needed: Patterns; 8-1/2- x 11-inch sheet of greeting card stock per card; size A2 matching envelopes; scraps of cotton/polyester fabrics—red, green and thin red and white stripe; scrap of fleece; glue stick; craft knife with sharp new blade; white marking pencil; red yarn and crewel embroidery needle; matching threads; standard sewing supplies.

Directions: Trace pattern to tracing paper and cut out. Fold card stock in half both ways, making sharp creases. Center pattern on front of card and lightly trace around it. Unfold card and cut out traced shape with craft knife.

Place pattern on fleece and trace around it. Cut out shape from fleece, cutting just inside the traced lines. Set fleece shapes aside.

HOLLY: Cut a 4- x 5-1/2-inch piece of green fabric. Place holly pattern on fabric and trace around it with white pencil. Cut left leaf off holly pattern and place within marked pattern on fabric. Trace center leaf edge on fabric. Hold fabric up to light and place holly-shaped fleece behind fabric. When shapes are matched up, pin the two together from the front. Using white thread, sew center leaf edge. Referring to pattern for placement and using green thread, sew leaf veins. Pull thread ends to back and clip close to fleece. Instructions for finishing the card are at end of directions.

STAR: Cut one 2-1/2- x 4-1/2-inch strip from green fabric and one from red fabric and, using 1/4-inch seam allowance, sew together along 4-1/2-inch edges.

Cut two 1-1/4- x 4-1/2-inch bias strips from striped fabric. Using 1/4-inch seam allowance and making sure that stripes match, sew strips together along 4-1/2-inch edge.

Press open seam allowances on both pieces. Cut striped piece in half widthwise. Fold corners of top edges to center seam; press. Unfold corners and cut off corners on pressed lines. You should now have two arrow-shaped striped pieces.

Referring to color photo, place arrow-shaped pieces on top of red/green piece so points touch in center. Baste striped pieces to red/green piece.

Hold fabric up to light and place fleece star behind fabric. When you're sure the shapes match, pin them together from the front. Using a satin zigzag stitch, applique the striped pieces onto the red/green piece, forming an X with your sewing. Pull thread ends to back and clip close to fleece.

TO FINISH: Open card and place fabric behind cutout on front. Close card, checking all seam lines and outlines of fleece against outlines of card cutout. When satisfied with placement, place card, face down, on clean surface and apply glue around edges of card cutout. Press fabric onto glue, making sure that the position has not changed.

Apply glue to that quadrant of the card which will cover the back side of the fabric and the remaining card area. Fold card in shape and place under heavy book until glue has thoroughly dried.✳

61

A Merry Christmas

By Mary Vaughn Armstrong
Spokane, Washington

AS SHE hung up the phone, Velma Ogeldorf leaned against the wall of the kitchen, determined that she wouldn't cry.

She'd been expecting the call all week, ever since taking "Panda" to the animal clinic. *Poor old cat,* she thought. *I couldn't let you go on coughing that way. I guess I knew you wouldn't be coming home…*

Velma closed her eyes and pictured the first time Panda had come home—tucked in the pocket of Harold's plaid shirt. That was 16 years ago, but it seemed like yesterday.

Silly old lady, she scolded herself. *She was only a cat. Made too much noise anyway. Still, it's a shame to lose her so soon after Harold…*

Velma shook her head, squared her shoulders and crossed the kitchen with resolute steps. She placed Panda's pretty blue bowl in the cupboard and closed the door. *No more cats,* she promised herself. *Losing them hurts too much.*

Eyeing the storage room, Velma remembered the string-tied boxes of ornaments and decorations. Christmas was only 10 days away, and she hadn't done a thing. *Maybe it would be best to forget about decorating this year…no sense in doing it just for myself. And all that baking—too much bother. Maybe it's time to simplify.*

Just then footsteps tramped on the front porch, and the doorbell chimed. When Velma answered its call, Donnie and Diane Zender, the 7-year-old twins from next door, peered up at her. Their cheeks were cranberry red from the wind.

"Hello, Mrs. Ogeldorf," Diane chirped, revealing a gap where her two front teeth had been. "We were just wondering if…" She paused. "You okay, Mrs. Ogeldorf?"

Velma cleared her throat. "I'm fine, Diane. What did you want?"

"We're selling mistletoe," Donnie piped up. "Seventy-five cents." He held up a bunch tied with red ribbon. "Would you like some?"

Velma sniffed. "Uh…I don't think so. Thank you."

Donnie looked puzzled. Diane nudged him and said, "We'll come back later, Mrs. Ogeldorf."

Velma nodded. "This isn't a very good time." She closed the door and sniffed again. *No sense in standing around,* she reproached herself. *I should get busy and clean the house. There's no sadness that hard work won't cure.*

She threw herself into the task, grateful for the diversion. Hours later, as she tossed her dust rags into the washing machine, the doorbell chimed again. Probably the twins with more mistletoe. This time she would say no and mean it.

"I said I didn't want—" Velma began, pulling the door open. She stopped. Behind the twins stood their mother, Ann. "I should have called you first, Velma," she apologized. "We've all just been caught up in the Christmas rush, and—"

Velma pushed open the screen door. "Come on in out of the cold." There was a moment of awkward silence as they all stood in the foyer. "Would you like to sit down?" she offered.

"Yes, thanks," Ann said, handing the box she'd been holding to Diane. "I should have come over before this, Velma, but…well, you know. Anyway, now I'm here to ask a big favor of you."

Velma's eyebrows raised. "Oh?"

Ann nodded. "Remember all the cookies you baked for the Women's Auxiliary Christmas party last year?"

Velma smiled. How could she forget? She'd worked for days on Lebkuchen, anise drops, meringue stars, springerle and trays of iced sugar cookies, cut with the cutters she'd used as a girl in her own mother's kitchen.

And now Ann was going to ask her to make them again this year. She turned the corners of her mouth down. "Ann, I've decided not to bake this year."

Ann held up a reassuring hand. "Oh no…we don't expect you to do that. We're hoping you'll agree to teach a cookie-baking class next year—unless those recipes are all family secrets!"

Velma caught her breath. "There

"Merry will be her name, because she's just what my Christmas needed."

is no secret. All it takes is practice. I learned by watching my mother, and she learned from her mother. But it takes time…"

"I'm sure that it does. The class would meet weekly for at least 6 months. After you've finished with cookies we'd all like to learn some of your other recipes. There'll be a budget for ingredients, and a small salary for teaching, too."

Velma looked away. She'd love to do it. But she'd promised herself she was going to simplify. Why get involved in such a big project?

Before she could say anything, a scratching sound echoed through the room, followed by a squeak. Ann grinned, and the children giggled. "Oh, we almost forgot," Ann said with a twinkle in her eyes. She nodded—and Diane reached down into the box and pulled out the fluffiest gray and white kitten that Velma had ever seen.

"Merry Christmas, Mrs. Ogeldorf!" Diane lisped, plopping the

for Mrs. Ogeldorf

bundle of fur in Velma's lap.

Velma gasped. "Whatever in the world…" Instinctively she stroked the kitten's back and felt its tiny body push against her hand. She scooped it in a ball and held it up to her face to peer into mischievous blue eyes just like Panda's.

Bewildered, Velma looked over at Ann. "You know about Panda?"

Ann knelt beside Velma's chair, scratching the kitten's head. "We found out this afternoon when we took 'Zip' to the clinic for his rabies shot. Dr. Cline felt terrible about Panda, but there was nothing he could do."

Ann's voice was warm with understanding. "We realize Panda can never be replaced. But 'Minnie' just had kittens again, and this one looks so much like Panda that, well…"

Velma stroked the little fluff ball while Ann and the twins waited for her to say something. Velma smiled. "Welcome home, 'Merry'," she declared, snuggling the kitten to her neck. "Merry will be her name, because she's just what my Christmas needed."

Ann gave her a hug and stood. "Come on, kids—time to start dinner." Velma lowered Merry to the floor and followed her guests to the front door.

"Thank you," she said. "And Merry Christmas to you, too!"

There was a new spring to Velma's step as she walked to the living room. Yawning, Merry crawled from beneath the overstuffed chair, and Velma began shaking with laughter. In spite of her feverish cleaning, a clump of lint hung rakishly over Merry's left ear.

"Come, my little friend," Velma said, scooping up the kitten and heading for the kitchen. "I'm going to give you some warm milk in a beautiful blue bowl. Then we've got to start getting things ready for Christmas…we'll hang the wreath tonight, and we'll start the baking tomorrow."

Velma stopped in her tracks. "Oh, dear," she said. "First I must make a phone call." She put Merry down and dialed the Zenders' number.

"Hello?"

"Ann, this is Velma. In all the excitement I forgot something. Tell the ladies to get their aprons ready —I'd love to teach that class!

"Oh, and one more thing…do you know of anywhere I could find some mistletoe?"

Merry Memories

WIDE-EYED about Christmas were Mildred Blue of Poland, New York and her cousin (left). "This photo was taken on a glass-plate negative in 1914, and the flash powder was lit with a match," Mildred recalls. "We were warned if we blinked we'd ruin the picture—and we made sure we didn't!"

NOW, THAT'S A SNOWMAN! Marilyn Brott of Plymouth, Wisconsin sent old photo (far left) of snowman with hat made of a 55-gal. drum and tire.

CHRISTMAS PAST is cherished by Vivian Nelson, Dassel, Minnesota. "The tree (center photo)—with real candles—came from our farm," she remembers. "That's me in the rocker (at far right), hugging my new doll."

ST. NICK 'N' BILLY. There were no reindeer near North Dakota in 1920. So this jolly old visitor (bottom left) had to improvise with a billy goat when stopping at Ole Ferguson's farm near Mayville, writes granddaughter Lael Thompson, Port Angeles, Washington.

SLEIGH BELLES. "In the early 30's, winter meant fewer chores and more time for fun," recounts Mrs. Robert Paltzer of Appleton, Wis. "On weekend afternoons, my sister, my cousin and I would hitch up the cutter and go for a ride. As you can see (below), even the dog came along with us!"

DECK THE HALLS

Words traditional

Traditional Welsh Melody

With spirit

1. Deck the halls with boughs of hol-ly,
2. See the blaz-ing Yule be-fore us, } Fa, la, la, la, la, la, la, la, la.
3. Fast a-way the old year pass-es,

'Tis the sea-son to be jol-ly,
Strike the harp and join the cho-rus, } Fa, la, la, la, la, la, la, la, la.
Hail the new, ye lads and lass-es,

Don we now our gay ap-par-el,
Fol-low me in mer-ry meas-ure, } Fa, la, la, la, la, la, la, la, la.
Sing we joy-ous all to-geth-er,

Troll the an-cient Yule-tide car-ol,
While I tell of Yule-tide treas-ure, } Fa, la, la, la, la, la, la, la, la.
Heed-less of the wind and weath-er,

Oh Christmas Tree

Over in the corner
Stands a special Christmas tree,
It's decorated with children's love,
It's there for all to see.
There's an angel made by Sarah
That sports a devilish grin,
A paper Santa Jessy made,
Beard missing from his chin.
A big red bow marks the year
Joe learned to tie his shoe,
And here's the faded star that
Ryan made when he was two.

It holds so many treasures
And priceless memories,
Of good times shared together
Beneath other Christmas trees.
It may not be too tall or straight,
The ornaments aren't new,
But in my eyes it's lovely
And no other tree would do.

Teri DeBlieck
Gerlaw, Illinois

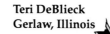

A Harvest of Winter Memories

These three families farm thousands of miles apart. But every Christmas, their acres of cut-your-own trees spread the same kind of old-fashioned joy!

HIKING OUT into the woods to claim a native pine is a Christmas tradition for many families. And thanks to a handful of far-apart farmers, the fun of finding the perfect tree is still making memories each holiday season.

"Cut-your-own-tree" farms are growing in popularity all across the country. And many offer more than farm-fresh evergreens.

Beverly and John Kayler of Cottonwood, Idaho have been raising trees on their place, "Fantasy Farms", for over 20 years.

"Our land is perfectly suited for growing pine seedlings," Beverly notes. "Most of the seedlings we raise are sold to other tree growers —but we've planted several thousand on our farm for Christmas customers, too."

With families flocking to the farm each Christmas, Beverly decided to open a shop offering seasonal decorations and ornaments. "I started off with $200 worth of stock—and sold it all in 2 days!" she says. "Since then the shop has gotten a little bigger each year."

Another Christmas tree farm is growing at the other end of the country. Elisabeth and Philip Jones —along with their son and his wife —run the "Jones Tree Farm" near Shelton, Connecticut.

"This farm has been in the Jones family for four generations," Elisabeth says. "We began as dairy farmers, selling just a few trees on the side. But then Philip found that he liked Christmas trees even better than cows."

Easterners have taken a liking to the taste of country the Joneses offer on their cut-your-own farm—*and* to the taste Elisabeth offers the family's customers. One year, she baked 25,000 cookies and 5,000 brownies for hungry holiday visitors!

"I started serving treats 30 years ago when a customer asked for a hot cup of coffee on a cold cutting day," she notes. "These days customers can sip coffee, cocoa or juice along with munching on my cookies. The kitchen is now three times bigger than when I began baking. But, even so, the cookies run out long before the customers do!"

A third farm never short on loyal Christmas customers is "Evergreen Acres" near East Troy, Wisconsin. Ann and Bob Feucht took over the farm 11 years ago. But they've only recently seen the final fruits of their year-round labor—from the time a seedling is planted till it's ready for Christmas trimming, as many as 10 years must pass.

"We *are* busy all year, trimming and working on the trees," Ann confirms. "We've never been busier, though, than when we first bought this farm. The few pine trees growing here then had *never* been trimmed!

"I remember one tree especially well. It was 10 feet tall...and must have been 10 feet wide, too. But we had a customer who thought it was beautiful, and that's all that counts."

Along with their trees, Ann also makes festive fresh wreaths every year. Another "service", however, has been offered only once.

"A local church needed two very tall, slender trees as Christmas decorations," Ann recalls with a smile. "We had just the right pair—but there was one problem. One of the trees had a large bald spot.

"So, with the blessings of the pastor—and a saw, hammer and nails—we cut a few boughs from a third tree and covered up the spot. The trees ended up looking identical ...even from the front pew!"

Ann and Bob still chuckle over that memory while they help make modern-day, last-a-lifetime memories for their cut-your-own customers. As with the Kaylers and the Joneses, their crop commands the public's attention for only a short time each year. But when it does, it fills hundreds of hearts with happiness.

CROCHET A FLURRY OF FLAKES!

DECK THE HALLS and trim the tree with the delicate filigree of crocheted snowflakes...you'll *love* the lacy way they look!

We've provided directions for three different versions of these six-sided beauties. Add a few of these flakes among your other ornaments—or crochet up a snowstorm and make enough to fill an entire tree!

CROCHETED SNOWFLAKES

Materials needed: One ball of white crochet cotton, size 10; No. 8 steel crochet hook; size 24 tapestry needle; rustproof straight pins; spray starch; paper towels; waxed paper; white glue; small sponge brush; translucent fishing line for hangers; 14-inch square piece of corrugated cardboard.

Finished size: Snowflakes measure from 4 to 6 inches.

Directions:
SNOWFLAKE NO. 1: Ch 7, join with sl st to form a ring.
Round 1: Ch 3, work 2 dc in ring; * ch 3, work 3 dc in ring; repeat from * four more times; end with ch 3, sl st in top of beg ch-3.
Round 2: Sl st in each of next 2 dc; in next ch-3 space work sl st, ch 3, 2 dc, ch 3, 3 dec, ch 1; * in next ch-3 space work 3 dc, ch 3, 3 dc, ch 1; repeat from * four more times; sl st in top of beg ch-3.
Round 3: Turn work over and sl st in ch-1 space just made; turn work back over to right side of work and * ch 3; in next ch-3 space work 3 dc, ch 3, 3 dc; ch 3, sl st in next ch-1 space; repeat from * five more times.
Round 4: Sl st in each of next 3 chs; ch 1; * sc in each of next 3 dc; work as follows in next ch-3 space; sc [ch 2, hdc in second ch from hook, ch 2, sl st in same space as hdc] three times, sl st in base of first hdc to secure, sc; sc in each of next 3 dc, ch 9; repeat from * five more times; end with sl st in beg sc. Use tapestry needle to weave in loose ends.

SNOWFLAKE NO. 2: Ch 7, join with sl st to form a ring.
Round 1: Ch 3, work 2 dc in ring; * ch 3, work 3 dc in ring; repeat from * four more times; end with ch 3, sl st in top of beg ch-3.
Round 2: Sl st in top of next 2 dc; in next ch-3 space sl st, work ch 3, 2 dc, ch 3, 3 dc; ch 11, sl st in fourth ch from hook, ch 7; * in next ch-3 space work 3 dc, ch 3, 3 dc; ch 11, sl st in fourth ch from hook, ch 7; repeat from * four more times; sl st in top of beg ch-3.
Round 3: Sl st in top of next 2 dc; * in next ch-3 space work sl st, ch 3, 2 dc, ch 3, sl st, ch 3, 2 dc, ch 3, sl st; sl st in top of each of next 3 dc; in next ch-7 space work 8 sc; in next ch-4 space work sl st, ch 3, dc, ch 2, sc, ch 3, trc, ch 3, sc, ch 2, dc, ch 3, sl st; in next ch-7 space work 8 sc; sl st in top of next 3 dc; repeat from * five more times; end with sl st in beg sl st. Use tapestry needle to weave in loose ends.

SNOWFLAKE No. 3: Ch 7, join with sl st to form a ring.
Round 1: Ch 3, work 2 dc in ring; * ch 3, work 3 dc in ring; repeat from * four more times; end with ch 3, sl st in top of beg ch-3.
Round 2: Sl st in next dc; * ch 2; in next ch-3 space work 3 dc, ch 7, sl st in sixth ch from hook, ch 1, 3 dc; ch 2, skip next dc, sl st in next dc; repeat from * five more times.
Round 3: Sl st in each of next 2 ch; ch 1, * sc in each of next 3 dc; sc in next ch-1 space; in next ch-6 space work sl st, ch 3, 3 dc, ch 2, sc, ch 2, dc, ch 2, sc, ch 3, trc, ch 3, sc, ch 2, dec, ch 2, sc, ch 2, 3 dc, ch 3, sl st; sc in next ch-1 space; sc in each of next 3 dc, ch 6, hdc in second ch from hook, ch 2, sl st in same space as hdc, ch; repeat from * five more times; end with sl st in beg sc and fasten off. Use tapestry needle to weave in loose ends.

STIFFENING: Cover corrugated cardboard with three layers of paper towels. Use rustproof straight pins to pin down all points of snowflake. Heavily spray snowflake with spray starch. Do not remove pins until snowflake is completely dry.

Place snowflake on a small piece of waxed paper. Use damp sponge brush to press glue straight from the squeeze bottle into snowflake. Place snowflake on clean piece of waxed paper and allow to dry completely. Make hanger from fishing line. ✳

LITTLE LOVE BIRDS ORNAMENT

IF you're looking for a unique ornament for your tree—or to give as a gift
—consider this cross-stitched project.
Backstitching and French knots add
the finishing touches to this charming
ornament.

FOLK ART LOVE BIRDS

Materials needed: Chart; heart pattern;
tracing paper; pencil; 8-inch square of white
14-count Aida cloth; 6-inch square of fabric
for backing; DMC six-strand embroidery
floss in colors listed on color key; size 24
tapestry needle; scrap of matboard or cardboard; scrap of polyester fleece; 1/2 yard of
red 1/2-inch-wide crocheted trim; 1/2 yard
of white 3/8-inch-wide scalloped edging; 8
inches of white 1/8-inch-wide satin ribbon;
white craft glue.

Directions: Referring to the color key
and chart, cross-stitch design on Aida cloth.
Separate six-strand floss and use three
strands for all cross-stitches. Refer to para-
graph below color key to work backstitches.

A three-quarter cross-stitch is occasionally used to round off part of the design. The
stitch will appear on the chart like this ◪, ◪,
◩ or ◲. The diagonal line shows the directions of the half cross-stitch and the symbol
indicates the color of the floss as well as the
direction of the quarter cross-stitch.

When stitching is complete, block stitched
piece.

Trace heart pattern to tracing paper, tracing both line No. 1 and line No. 2. Cut out
pattern on line No. 2. Place pattern on back
of stitched piece so design is centered within line No. 1, and trace around line No. 2.
Also trace around line No. 2 on wrong side
of backing fabric. Cut out each piece along
line No. 2.

Cut away pattern to line No. 1. Center
pattern on wrong side of each piece and
trace around it. Clip edges of both pieces
almost to line No. 1.

Trace around pattern twice on fleece and
twice on cardboard. Cut on traced lines.

Place stitched piece with wrong side up
on work surface. Place fleece in center, then
place cardboard on top. Apply a thin layer of
glue around edge of cardboard. Bring clipped
edges of stitched piece up over cardboard
edges and press onto glued surface.

Glue scalloped edging around edge of
cardboard so scallops extend just beyond
edge of stitched piece. Glue red trim behind
white edging. You may have to clip the base
edges of the trims to make them more flexible.

Layer backing, fleece and cardboard as
you did with stitched piece. Glue the clipped
backing edge to cardboard. Fold 8-inch
piece of satin ribbon in half to form loop and
glue ends of loop to top of cardboard. Glue
cardboard pieces together.✳

COLOR KEY	DMC
⊞ White	
✕ Dk. Christmas Red	498
▼ Christmas Red	321
⊡ Med. Delft Blue	799
⊟ Dk. Delft Blue	798
▩ Royal Blue	797
✳ Lt. Tangerine	742
O Med. Yellow	743
● Med. Parrot Green	906
Black	310

Backstitching: Outline birds and
birds' eyes with single strand of 310;
curving lines with single strand of 906;
tulip stem with three strands of 906.

Loop extends
outward

Back of
ornament

Three-quarter cross-stitches

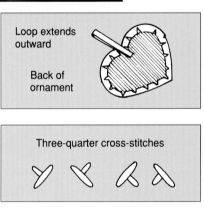

Line 1

Line 2

Clip

GARLAND OF COWS LOOKS MOOVELOUS

TO ADD an "amoosing" touch to your holiday decor, why not try this merry garland of Holstein cows? Here's an extra bonus: You can make the garland as long as you like to fit your mantel or Christmas tree.

Leave open

HOLSTEIN GARLAND

Materials needed: Pattern; tracing paper; pencil; lightweight cotton fabrics—1/8 yard white and 1/8 yard black; 2 yards of 5/8-inch-wide green grosgrain ribbon; polyester stuffing; small amount of black embroidery floss; water-soluble marker; white tailor's chalk; standard sewing supplies.

Directions: Trace cow pattern to tracing paper and cut out. Trace each of the spots separately to tracing paper and cut out.

Cut six 4-1/2- x 5-1/2-inch rectangles from white fabric. Using water-soluble marker, trace around cow pattern on three of the white rectangles, having the cows all go in the same direction. Do *not* cut the cows out yet.

Using white tailor's chalk, trace a bunch of the spots onto the black fabric. Add 1/8-inch seam allowance around each spot as you cut them out.

Referring to photo, randomly pin some spots on each cow shape. Turn under raw edges as you hand-applique each spot in place with black thread.

Pin appliqued cow right side down on top of plain white rectangle. The marked shape of the cow should show through to wrong side of fabric. If markings do not show through, baste along the outline and then use the basting line as your stitch guide.

Machine-stitch on the marked lines, leaving opening where indicated on pattern. Cut out each cow, cutting about 1/8 inch from stitched edges. Before turning cow right side out, push in the head and legs. Turn cow right side out by pulling head through opening first, then continue to pull on cow's head so body follows. Using blunt end of toothpick or skewer, gently push out ears and udders.

Stuff each cow and neatly hand-sew openings closed. Using all six strands in the needle, embroider a short straight stitch with black embroidery floss for each cow's eye.

Using a damp sponge, remove any visible water-soluble lines. Tack the cows together with white thread. Cut two 1-yard lengths of grosgrain ribbon. Fold each length in half. Tack folded edge of one ribbon behind head of first cow; tack folded edge of second ribbon behind back end of last cow. Tie each set of ribbons into a bow. ✳

SPEEDY STOCKING STUFFERS: Fill a pocket-size photo book with snapshots of a special outing or vacation.

● Think of hobbies and stuff stockings accordingly: stamps, sewing scissors, hair ribbons, after-shave, sweet soaps, crayons, candy canes, small toys, etc.

● Wrap a bar of scented soap in nylon netting tied with ribbon for a fragrant air freshener.

● Make bookmarks out of leather, felt or fabric to fit the person's interests.

● Glue tiny seashells onto small boxes for "whatnot" containers.

● Print up a stack of "IOU's" for a variety of services; include a gift certificate for dinner at your place some night.

● Glue fabric on the cover of a purse-size note pad and include a small pencil.

● Paint a rock for a decorative paperweight. Use your imagination!

● Use leftover yarn to knit doll clothes, pot holders, coffee cup coasters or a pair of mittens.

HO-HO HOLIDAY ORNAMENTS

MUCH of the fun of crafting Christmas ornaments is anticipating how they'll look on the tree and knowing that they'll be displayed and cherished year after year. This pair of cross-stitched ornaments framed by twigs is bound to become a tree-trimming tradition in many country homes.

CROSS-STITCHED ORNAMENTS

COLOR KEY	DMC
⊡ White	
☒ Bright Christmas Red	666
☑ Lt. Peach Flesh	754
◉ Med. Garnet	815
♥ Med. Brown	433
☑ Dk. Christmas Green	895
◥ Med. Topaz	782
▣ Vy. Lt. Ultra Tan	739
N Rose	335
⊟ Bright Christmas Green	700
Black	310

ALPHABET CHART

```
ABCDEFGHIJKLM
NOPQRSTUVWXYZ
1234567890
```

CROSS-STITCHED ORNAMENTS

Materials needed: FOR EACH PROJECT: Chart; 3-1/2- x 3-3/4-inch piece of Charles Craft 18-count Fiddler's cloth; DMC six-strand embroidery floss in colors listed on color key; size 24 tapestry needle; 6-inch length of dark green rattail cord; 2-3/8- x 2-3/4-inch piece of cardboard; two 2-1/4-inch-long x 1/4-inch-diameter twigs; two 2-3/4-inch-long x 1/4-inch-diameter twigs; glue gun; glue stick. FOR MERRY CHRISTMAS: Small piece of graph paper; pencil.

Directions: Hand-overcast or zigzag raw edges of cloth to prevent raveling. Fold cloth in half, fold in half again to determine center; mark this point. To find center of chart, draw lines across chart, connecting arrows. Begin stitching at this point so design will be centered.

ANTIQUE SANTA: Separate six-strand floss and use two strands for all cross-stitches. Backstitch, where indicated with heavy lines, with one strand black floss, except for stripes in candy cane, backstitch these with two strands 666. Make doll's hair and eyes with French knots: one strand of black floss wrapped twice around needle.

MERRY CHRISTMAS: Separate six-strand floss and use two strands for all cross-stitches. Backstitch "Merry Christmas" with one strand 700. Using alphabet chart, work out family name on graph paper. Backstitch name with one strand 666.

To finish project, mount finished piece on cardboard with glue stick. Using glue gun, glue one short twig to top of design, flush with right edge. Glue long twig to right side of design, flush with bottom edge. Continue around outer edge of design with remaining twigs. Fold rattail cord in half to form hanging loop and glue to cardboard backing. ✱

ANTIQUE SANTA CHART

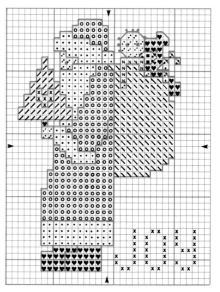

MERRY CHRISTMAS CHART

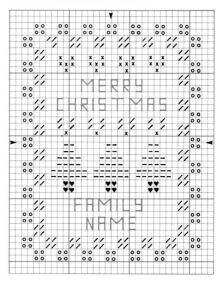

FLORAL CHRISTMAS CARDS: Press flowers and foliage between pages of a heavy book. When dry, arrange petals and leaves on a notecard and carefully cover with clear contact paper. Trim edges and write a personal sentiment on the back.

'BELLS' FOR BOUGHS

TRIMMING the tree is sure to be a happy celebration when you create these easy-to-make ornaments.

STENCILED ORNAMENTS

Materials needed: (For four ornaments) Patterns; tracing paper; pencil; 9- x 12-inch piece of 22-count white evenweave cross-stitch fabric; 9- x 12-inch piece of red felt; red stencil paint; small stencil brush; 6-inch square of stencil mylar; craft knife; black fine-point permanent marker; red six-strand embroidery floss; embroidery needle; 2-5/8 yards of 1/8-inch-wide red satin ribbon; 1/2 yard of 1/8-inch-wide white satin ribbon; 3 yards of red rattail cord; 12 small jingle bells; four small clapper bells; 34 green seed beads; beading needle or No. 8 sharp needle; polyester stuffing; fabric glue; standard sewing supplies.

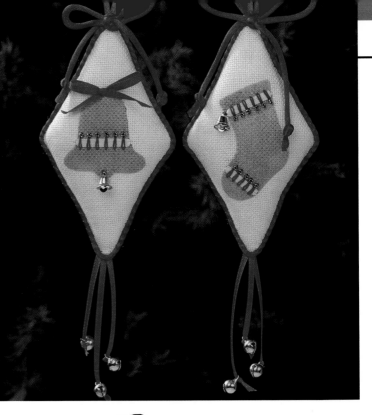

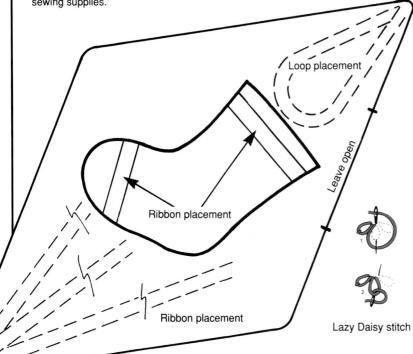

Lazy Daisy stitch

Directions: Using black fine-point marker, trace stocking and bell patterns to mylar, making sure to leave enough space between each shape to accommodate the stencil brush. Using craft knife, cut away each shape.

Trace diamond pattern to tracing paper and cut out. Using pattern, trace four diamonds on cross-stitch fabric (make sure they're on the straight of grain) but do not yet cut them out.

Referring to photo for placement, position stencil over one diamond so design is well positioned. Using red stencil paint and stencil brush, stencil bell shape in center of two diamonds and boot shape in two diamonds.

Thread white satin ribbon into an em-

broidery needle. On one bell ornament, come up at point A, leaving 1/2-inch end of ribbon in back of fabric. Bring ribbon across width of bell, making sure it didn't twist, and bring needle down at point B. Cut ribbon, leaving 1/2-inch end on wrong side of fabric. Repeat this with the second bell ornament and with the two boot ornaments where indicated on pattern. Secure all ribbon ends to back of fabric with a dab of fabric glue.

Separate red six-strand floss and use two strands to span the width of each ribbon with lazy Daisy stitches. Using a beading needle or No. 8 sharp needle and green thread, attach a green seed bead to each lazy Daisy stitch. Cut out each diamond on the traced line.

For each ornament, cut one 3-inch, one 3-1/2-inch, one 4-inch and one 8-inch length of red satin ribbon. Refer to pattern for placement of ribbons. Fold 8-inch length in half, forming a loop, and pin to top on right side of stenciled diamond, raw edges matching and loop facing center of diamond. Pin three remaining ribbons to bottom on right side of diamond, raw edges matching and uneven ends facing center of diamond.

With right sides together and 1/4-inch seam allowance, sew felt diamond to stenciled diamond, leaving opening for turning where indicated on pattern. Clip seam allowances at corners and turn diamond right side out.

Cut rattail cord into four equal lengths. Place center of one length of cord at bottom of diamond and tack to secure. Whipstitch cord to outside edge of diamond, ending with long ends at top. Tie long ends into a bow.

For each bell ornament, cut a 9-inch length of red satin ribbon, tie ribbon into a bow and tack bow to top of stenciled bell. Tack a clapper bell to center bottom of each stenciled bell and to left top corner of each stenciled stocking.

Thread a jingle bell onto each satin ribbon that extends from bottom of ornament. Secure bell to ribbon by knotting end of ribbon.✼

FLORAL FLAIR

TOPPED WITH satin ribbon and silk roses, these delicate floral ornaments add a touch of Victorian charm to a tree. You can make them for yourself...for a keepsake for a friend...or even as a special take-along hostess gift during the holidays.

VICTORIAN ORNAMENTS

Materials needed: (For one ornament) One 2-1/2-inch-diameter glass or satin Christmas ball; five 3/4-inch-diameter silk roses; three 1-inch-long artificial leaves; baby's breath; 6-inch piece of cloth-covered florist's wire; 2 yards of 1/8-inch-wide satin ribbon; Aleene's Designer tacky glue.

Directions: Remove metal cap and hanger from glass ball. Discard the hanger but not the metal cap. Cut a 12-inch piece of ribbon and thread through hole or holes in cap so both ends are on inside of cap. Tie ribbon ends together in a knot.

If a satin ball is used, tie ribbon ends to metal loop at top of ball or, if there is no metal loop, glue ribbon ends directly to top of ball.

Hold remaining 1-2/3 yards of ribbon with thumb and forefinger of left hand, about 6 inches from one end. Use next 2 inches of long end to form a 1-inch loop. Hold loop in place with same thumb and forefinger. Do not let go of the 6-inch length. Make a second loop on other side of thumb in same manner. Continue to make 1-inch loops until you have six loops on each side of bow.

Use next 12 inches of ribbon to make one 6-inch loop beneath smaller loops, and

let it hang down. Let 6 inches of remaining ribbon hang down and trim off excess if necessary. Bring wire over center of bow and gather loops forward.

Turn bow over and twist wire to secure loops in place. Do not cut ends of wire. Cut open 6-inch loop to make streamers. There should now be a total of four 6-inch streamers. Use blade of scissors to curl ribbon. Trim ends as desired.

Using ends of wire, attach bow to top of metal cap, just below hanging loop. Trim wire ends. Put bead of glue along top open edge of glass ball, and replace cap on ball. Fluff out bow. On satin ball, attach bow to metal loop or, if there is no loop, to top of ball.

Cut stems of flowers and baby's breath short. Glue flowers among loops of bow and around top edge of ball. Glue leaves and baby's breath between flowers and loops of ribbon. Fill in with baby's breath.✳

Tie center with wire

Cut here

SPICE UP THE SEASON!

HERE'S a fun family project that can add a "delicious" touch to your tree. Be forewarned, though. These cinnamon-scented ornaments look and smell like cookies but they're NOT EDIBLE. Be sure to caution unsuspecting family members and keep them out of the reach of pets and small children.

CRAFTY COOKIE ORNAMENTS

Materials needed: (For eight 6-inch-tall or-naments) 1 cup ground cinnamon; 1 table-spoon ground cloves; 1 tablespoon ground nutmeg; 3/4 cup applesauce; 2 tablespoons

Aleene's Tacky Glue; 10 yards 1/2-inch-wide ribbon.

Directions: In a medium bowl, combine cinnamon, cloves and nutmeg. Stir in apple-sauce and glue. Work mixture with hands for 2 to 3 minutes to form a ball. If mixture is too dry, add more applesauce; if too wet, add more cinnamon.

Knead the ball on a cinnamon-sprinkled surface until it holds together well. Divide into 4 equal portions and roll out each 1/4 inch thick. Cut dough with cookie cutters into various shapes. Place on cookie sheets.

Use a pencil to make a small hole in the top of each for hanging ribbon. Be sure the hole goes all the way through. Air-dry orna-ments. Turn over from time to time to ensure even drying. (It will take about 4-5 days.) For faster results, place in sunlight or dry in a warm oven (250°-300°) for several hours.

When ornaments are dry, insert ribbon—cut into 22-inch lengths—through hole and tie ends into a knot. Tie another length into a bow around first ribbon near ornament top.✳

JINGLE BELLS

J. PIERPONT

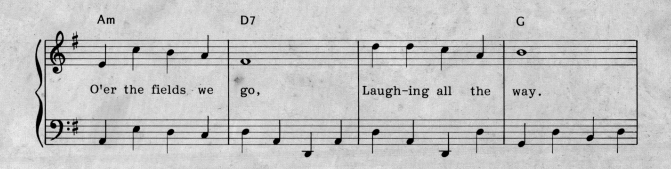

Dash-ing through the snow, In a one horse o - pen sleigh,

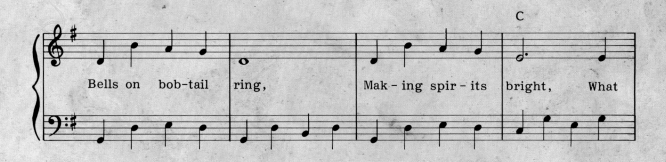

O'er the fields we go, Laugh-ing all the way.

Bells on bob-tail ring, Mak-ing spir - its bright, What

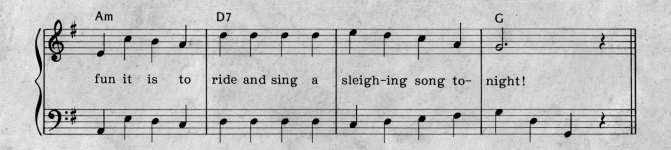

fun it is to ride and sing a sleigh-ing song to- night!

Refrain

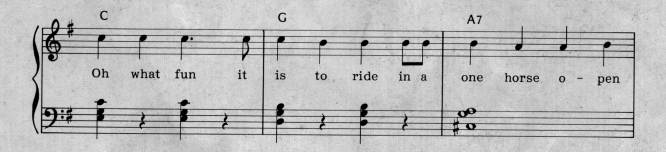

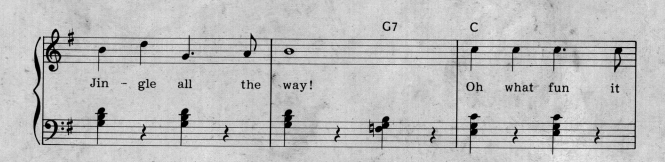

"Hi ho...hi ho...to Grandma's house we go!"

The Cardinal Tree

By Sharma Krauskopf, Lansing, Michigan

I HAD driven to our small cabin up in the north woods with my dog, "Natasha", to get away from the holiday rush for a day. Not too long after I arrived, I found myself completely snowed in—on Christmas Eve!

A call home confirmed that the roads were impassable. Promising my husband, Tom, and our girls I'd be there as soon as the plow got through, I resolved to make the best of things. After all, our small cabin had electricity, a dependable wood stove, lanterns and plenty of food. Spending the night was clearly better than taking the chance of becoming stranded on a blizzard-bound highway.

Still, it didn't take long for loneliness to set in. I knew the best defense was to keep myself busy, so I set about decorating the cabin...after all, it *was* Christmas Eve!

I bundled up, waded out into the storm and quickly cut a short, fat pine. Back in the cabin, with my Christmas tree thawing near the stove, I foraged for holiday trappings.

I began making plans for a personal Christmas Eve dinner: roast chicken, canned peas, potatoes, gravy and an apple pie. As I peeled some apples for the pie, I hummed along to Christmas carols on the radio.

With the pie in the oven, I turned my attention to trimming the little pine tree. I popped corn and managed to string enough of it to drape in festoons around the boughs, as the spicy aroma of apple pie filled the cabin.

Later, snug, warm and well-fed, but still feeling a little sorry for myself having to spend Christmas Eve alone, I was ready to settle in for my "long winter's nap". Natasha watched as I added a large hardwood log to the firs and piled three old-fashioned quilts on the bed.

Snuggled under their protection, I drowsily wondered about the animals in the woods. *Are they safe and protected from the storm? Do they know about Christmas?*

Through the window I could see that the storm had nearly ended, leaving the trees in the pine forest near the cabin dressed in fluffy white robes. As the clouds parted, moonlight embellished the scene with a million sparkling diamonds.

I noticed two bright-red cardinals fluttering to a perfectly shaped pine just outside my window. The moonlight was so bright I could see they were carrying sprigs of holly and garlands of berries to the tree.

Woodland Dream

A large owl landed on a hardwood nearby, and its summoning call echoed through the silent forest. It wasn't long before other creatures also came out from their snow-sheltered hiding

---

"Those cardinals had reminded me of what Christmas truly is..."

---

places—a pair of graceful white-tailed deer...a fat brown beaver...a mother raccoon and two frisky babies.

Grayish-brown rabbits appeared on the carpet of snow and hopped to join the group. Next, a brown and white coyote joined the gathering, and then a small black bear took a position on the largest log near the tree. The creatures all stood, poised and ready.

Suddenly, a brilliant star appeared in the sky, positioned just above the tip of the tree. The starlight radiated in all directions, flooding the gathering of animals with a shimmering, golden glow!

For a moment, the animals basked in that light, sharing a silent celebration and forgetting struggle and survival. Then, a sudden noise jolted them, and just as quickly as they had come, they disappeared back into their woodland homes...*Ring-g-gg!*

I jumped, startled out of a deep sleep by the ringing of the telephone. It was Tom and the girls calling to wish me Merry Christmas. When I told them how I had decorated the cabin, they decided to pack our presents and drive up to join me once the roads were cleared!

I rebuilt the fire and made coffee, then sat by the window as the sun rose. Not a track or mark disturbed the pristine quilt of snow laid over the world. The beauty and silence charmed and beckoned.

I donned warm clothing, put on my snowshoes and headed out to feed the birds. When I opened the door, a whitetail and her twin fawns lifted their heads in curiosity before prancing off. Seeing them made me remember my dream about the cardinals' Christmas tree!

Could that special tree really exist? With Natasha bounding along beside me, I set out for the little pine forest in search of it. I found it easily, right where I knew it would be. There were no garlands or holly... but there *were* two cardinals perched near the top of the tree—a scarlet echo of my dream.

I hadn't been alone after all on Christmas Eve! Instead, I'd been part of a very special celebration. Those cardinals had reminded me of what Christmas truly is: A time for every living creature to come together in peace and acceptance...a time to acknowledge and respect our differences...while joining together to worship and celebrate.

I couldn't wait to share Christmas in the country with Tom and the girls when they arrived. I had the feeling it would be our best ever!

Christmas Magic Returns... In Red

By Carolynn Comstock
Calumet, Wisconsin

MY POINSETTIA is dressed up in its holiday best—again!

Only months ago, not a hint of red shaded the green leaves...but now, brilliant bracts of scarlet surround all of the tiny yellow flower clusters. I marvel once more at the timely transformation—as miraculous as the very first time I witnessed it years ago at my grandmother's house...

Beneath the Christmas tree that year was a perky potted poinsettia with Grandma's name on it. How she grew to cherish that plant for brightening the long, white days of winter!

The following spring, however, Grandma's poinsettia faded—its leaves furling, then falling. But instead of simply tossing it out, as I had seen her do with other plants past their prime, Grandma carefully cut back the stems, repotted her poinsettia and placed it in a sunny spot on her back porch. Soon it was covered with bright green leaves.

Then, on an autumn evening chilly with the suggestion of a frost, Grandma retrieved her precious poinsettia and proclaimed, "Child, it's time to make some Christmas magic!"

Right after supper, before doing the dishes, Grandma placed that poinsettia in the very darkest corner of her hall closet. Wide-eyed, I watched as she tucked a bath towel along the bottom of the door so not a single ray of light could break through.

Next morning, after breakfast, she brought her poinsettia out into the light of day...but on that evening—and every evening thereafter—she closed it up tight in the closet.

After a few weeks, a magical change began to take place. Each day, a little more green was gone... replaced by red! By Thanksgiving Day, that poinsettia had come out of the closet to stay, promising a colorful Christmas just as Grandma had planned.

Now, as I coax my own poinsettia to renew itself for yet another Christmas, I delight again in its magical message. This pretty plant brings the promise of hope and new life to all who see it. During Christmastime in the country, could any promise be more perfect?

A BRIGHT BOUQUET

AS ELEGANT as any garden-grown flowers, these lacy craft carnations make an attractive bouquet for a holiday centerpiece. Or, you could give them to special friends who stop by —simply tie a single crimson carnation and a sprig of baby's breath together with a perky red bow for a holiday hello!

CROCHETED CARNATIONS

Materials needed: (For 12 carnations) J & P Coats Knit-Cro-Sheen 100% mercerized cotton—2 balls each of red and white (A) and 1 ball of green (B); twelve 12-inch lengths of No. 18 stem wire; green florist's tape; 12 artificial carnation leaves; No. 7 steel crochet hook; crewel needle; needle-nose pliers.

Gauge: 10 tr = 1 inch and 3 rounds = 1-1/4 inches.

Abbreviations:

ch	chain
sl st	slip stitch
tr	treble stitch
yo	yarn over
sc	single crochet

Directions:

FLOWER: Beginning at center of flower with A, ch 10. Join with sl st to form ring.
Round 1: Ch 4 (counts as 1 tr), 19 tr in ring —20 tr. Join with sl st to top of ch 4.
Round 2: Ch 4 (counts as 1 tr), tr in same place as sl st, 2 tr in each tr around—40 tr. Join with sl st to top of ch 4.
Rounds 3-4: Repeat round 2—160 tr.
Round 5: Sc in same place as sl st, * ch 10, sc in next tr; repeat from * around. Join with sl st to first sc. Cut thread and fasten.

CALYX: Beginning at center with B, ch 4. Join with sl st to form ring.
Round 1: 7 sc in ring. Do not join following rounds, but work in a spiral, placing a marker at beginning of each new round.
Round 2: 2 sc in each sc around—14 sc.
Round 3: * Sc in next sc, 2 sc in next sc; repeat from * around—21 sc.
Rounds 4-10: Sc in each sc around. Cut thread and fasten.

TO FINISH: Sew a running stitch with A thread through the second round of the flower. Pull thread tight to gather flower. Knot ends to secure. Place flower in calyx so bottom of flower is at bottom of calyx. Pin in place and hand-sew the two together with B thread and an overcast stitch. Spread flower so edges overlap calyx.

Double-loop one end of a length of wire. Insert other end of wire through center of flower and calyx and pull down. Holding flower in place, fold one leaf in half and hold against calyx and the stem wire. Wrap florist's tape several times around base of calyx to secure leaf, then wrap remaining stem. ✻

COUNTRY CHARM

STUFFED PILLOW WREATH

Materials needed: Fabric scraps—1/6 yard each of three different holiday prints; 10-inch wire box wreath (see illustration); 14 yards of 1/4-inch-wide satin ribbon (all one color or several coordinating colors); polyester stuffing; potpourri or scented oils; standard sewing supplies.

Directions: Make 13 pillows of each print for a total of 39 pillows. For each pillow, cut a 3-1/2- x 4-inch piece of fabric. Fold fabric in half lengthwise with right sides together; 3-1/2-inch edges should meet. Using 1/8-inch seam allowance, sew one end and one side, leaving other end open for stuffing.

Turn pillow right side out and stuff loosely, adding some potpourri or scented oils to the stuffing of some of the pillows. Tuck in raw ends of openings and neatly hand-sew pillows closed.

Using 12- to 13-inch lengths of ribbon, tie pillows to wreath as follows: Tie one pillow to two center wires. Tie a second pillow to one side of first pillow, catching ribbon around one center wire and the outside wire. Tie a third pillow to opposite center wire and the inside wire. Proceed all around wreath in this manner, alternating prints until wreath is covered.

The wreath can also be used as a table decoration with a candle in the center. ✻

YOUR HOME will announce your Christmas welcome in country style when you make this wreath of tiny stuffed pillow packages.

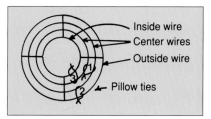

- Inside wire
- Center wires
- Outside wire
- Pillow ties

CHRISTMAS CRECHE FOR KIDS

THIS Nativity is one anyone can make and everyone (even the little ones in your home) will enjoy. In fact, the figures are made with little tots in mind, so get out your felt, scissors and glue and create this colorful manger scene for the holiday season!

"PLEASE TOUCH" NATIVITY SCENE

Materials needed: Patterns; tracing paper; pencil; black embroidery floss; invisible sewing thread (available at fabric stores); tacky glue; small dried beans (great northern beans are best); good-quality heavy felt—deep blue, bright blue, light blue, brown, tan, yellow, white, bright pink, red, green, purple, fuchsia, coral, pastel green or blue, light beige, light pink, gold, lavender, black and brown; standard sewing supplies.

Directions: Outer robe A and inner robe B are used for all the figures except the Angel and Baby Jesus. Faces, arms and head pieces are glued to these figures according to individual directions below.

Faces: Using light pink felt, cut out faces and hands for Mary, Angel and Baby Jesus. Cut all other faces and hands from light beige.

Eyes: Baby Jesus' eyes are French knots of two strands black embroidery floss with one twist. All other eyes are half-moon shapes of black felt. Glue all eyes in place and take one stitch through each with black thread for extra hold.

Bodies: Glue each figure's trims to its body front. Place each front, with right side up, on matching backing piece and pin layers to prevent shifting. Using invisible thread, stitch an 1/8-inch seam around the figure, leaving bottom open. Trim seam allowances close to stitching. The seams will be on the outside of the body so don't turn them.

Spread bottom opening of figure and stand on a matching piece of felt. Cut bottom piece of felt large enough so it extends 1/2 inch around bottom of figure.

Baste pieces together close to the edge. Machine-stitch 1/8-inch seam with invisible thread, leaving 1-inch opening in back. Fill figure with dried beans until almost full. Hand-sew opening closed with invisible thread. Trim seam allowances close to seam.

MARY: Glue light blue inner robe A to bright blue outer robe A, matching bottom and right edges. Glue face, brown hair and hood in place. Glue hand and sleeve in place, making sure hand has the thumb up. Decorate Mary's dress with red heart and two green teardrop shapes.

SHEPHERD: Use the same pattern pieces as Mary, using tan felt, and trim as shown in the photo.

JOSEPH: Glue bright blue inner robe B to deep blue outer robe A, matching bottom and left edges. Glue face, hand, sleeve and hood in place. Glue a red band on the hood.

For lantern: Cut one pattern piece of gold and glue a small piece of light blue behind lantern opening. Cut small strip for candle, and small yellow flame. Glue both to the blue in the opening. Glue the lantern handle to Joseph's hand.

BABY JESUS: Glue yellow hay piece to crib, using photo for placement. Glue the white pillow, pink face, blanket and tan footboard in place. Add tiny pink hands in place on the blanket and coral halo above the head. Add red hearts and green teardrops to crib.

ANGEL: Glue the pink hands to sleeves and set aside. Glue the pink face to the white

80

front. Trim the hair with scalloped pinking shears and glue in place. Add curl to middle of forehead. Place the sleeves so the hands come together in prayer. Glue just the sleeves. Place halo and wings behind the backing and glue in place. Decorate the Angel's dress with a pink heart and pastel green teardrop shapes at lower center.

THREE WISE MEN: Cut out and decorate jar, pitcher and box for gifts and set aside.

WISE MAN FACING RIGHT: Glue yellow inner robe B to red outer robe A with bottom and left edges even. Glue red cloak to left side. To this backing add the light beige face, hand, sleeve, head piece, crown and mustache.

WISE MAN FACING LEFT: Glue fuchsia inner robe B to purple outer robe A with bottom and right edges even. Glue purple cloak to the right side. Add the other pieces same as above directions.

WISE MAN FACING FRONT: Center yellow inner robe B to green outer robe A and glue. Add green cloak panels to outer edges and glue. Cut green cap where indicated on pattern and glue in place to coral headdress. Add the pieces to the backing as above.

Decorate the sleeves and robes of the Wise Men with colorful strips of felt. Glue a gift to the hands of each Wise Man.✳

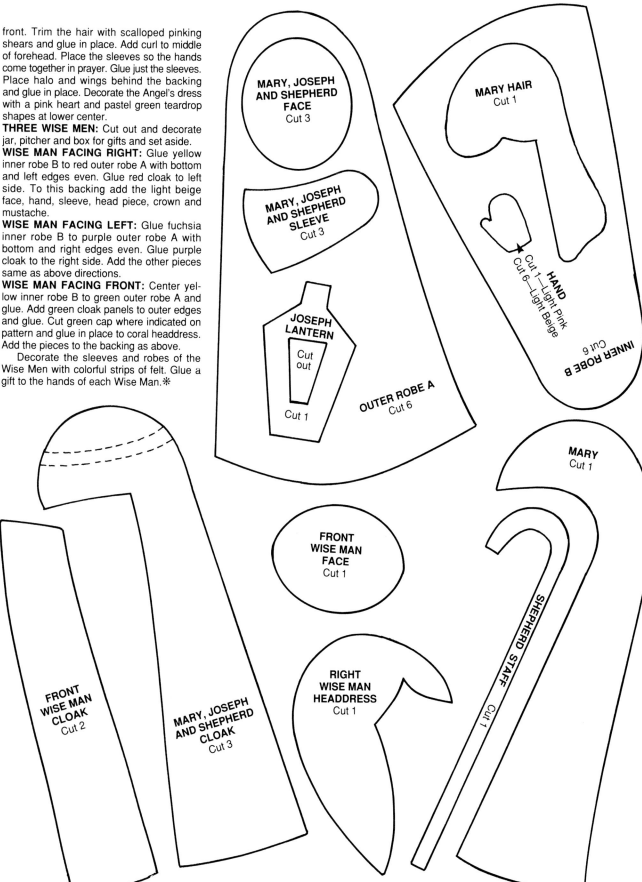

WELCOME WREATHS

FOR old-fashioned Christmas beauty, try nature's bounty! You can make this simple twine wreath (left) to hang on the tree, to trim a package or to use with your holiday table decorations. And the grapevine wreath (below left) adds country charm to a window or door.

BALING TWINE MINI-WREATH

Materials needed: Three 14-inch lengths of baling twine; small piece of florist's wire; 1/3 yard of 1/4-inch-wide ribbon.

Directions: Leaving 1 inch of twine unbraided at beginning and end, braid the three lengths of baling twine together. Overlap the ends and secure with wire. Fray the 1-inch ends of the twine a little. Conceal the wire with a ribbon bow. Trim away any loose "hairs" of the twine, and your mini-wreath is ready to hang on the tree or trim a package. ✳

GRAPEVINE WREATH

Materials needed: 5-foot lengths of wild grapevine; string or twine; brown cloth-covered florist's wire; gloves; scissors; natural materials for decoration such as dried milkweed pods, wheat, oats, baby's breath, statice and bittersweet; ribbon.

Directions: Begin by gathering wild grapevines that grow high up into trees and along country fences. The best vines for working measure about 1/2 inch in diameter. Grapevines should be harvested in the fall when the leaves are off, or in the spring before the vines bud out.

Using gloves to protect your hands, break off the vines a foot or two from the ground. Check to make sure that you have a live vine. (Dead vines are impossible to coil as they snap easily.) Keep your head down, or wear safety glasses, when pulling vines from a tree. It will take two or three vines to make a wreath or basket, depending on their length.

If you can't use the vines right away, store them in a dark, cool place. If you must store them longer than a month, soak them in water for about 1 hour before using them.

Start wreath by making a circle of the thickest part of the vine and weaving loose end around to secure a framework. Continue to coil vine over original circle and slightly outward. Weave in the next vine and continue until wreath is desired size. For best appearance, wreath should be 4 inches or more in width when complete. Tie vines in place with string or twine.

Allow the wreath to sit for a couple of days before you completely secure the vines in four to six places with brown cloth-covered wire.

Decorate the wreath with natural materials and ribbon as desired. ✳

HOLIDAY HARVEST

TO ADD a natural touch to a country-flavored Christmas table setting, bring in the sheaves, then weave some easy napkin rings—with wheat!

WHEAT NAPKIN RINGS

Materials needed: Twelve 12-inch wheat straws with heads attached; short length of ribbon; string.

Directions: Using string, tie straws together just below the heads. Divide the straws into two equal parts. Hold half in one hand and half in the other hand. Have another person hold the heads, or tie them to a doorknob.

Beginning with the right hand, give the straws three complete twists (wrist motion is toward the inside). Take the left-hand straws, carry over the right-hand straws. Change hands.

Again, give the straws in the right hand three complete twists. Carry left-hand straws over the right-hand straws. Change hands. Keep constant tension on the strands and twist with the same even motion. Twist until sufficient length is reached to make a ring for a napkin. Tie off end. Shape into a ring and tie end next to wheat heads. ✳

GROW A TINY TREE!

YOUR CHILDREN will be eager to help you decorate for the holidays when you get them started on fun, festive projects like this miniature fabric tree. There's no sewing involved—just a simple pattern plus scissors, pins and a few other materials.

NO-SEW MINIATURE TREE

Materials needed: Pattern; tracing paper; pencil; 6-inch Styrofoam tree form; 1/2 yard fabric; 1/4 yard matching fabric; short stick pins.

Directions: Trace pattern to tracing paper and cut out. Using traced pattern, cut 45 hexagons from 1/2 yard fabric and 16 hexagons from matching fabric.

Fold hexagons in half and press (see Fig. 1). Next, fold side edges to center so they meet, and press. Cut the top points even with the straight edge (see Fig. 2).

With point facing down and smooth side out, pin pieces around bottom of tree shape, overlapping side corners slightly (see Fig. 3).

Place second row of pieces around tree, overlapping first row. Continue in this manner to top of tree, randomly inserting matching color pieces. Fold the raw edges of the top piece to the inside so you'll have a nice smooth finish. ✳

FIG 1

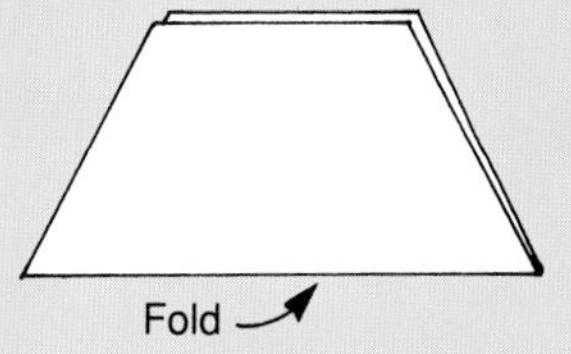

Fold

FIG 2

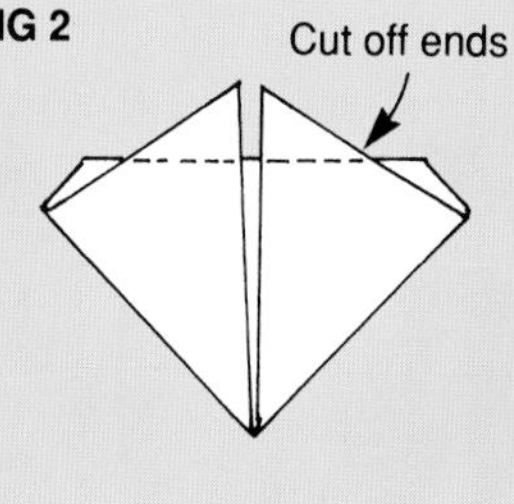

Cut off ends

FIG 3

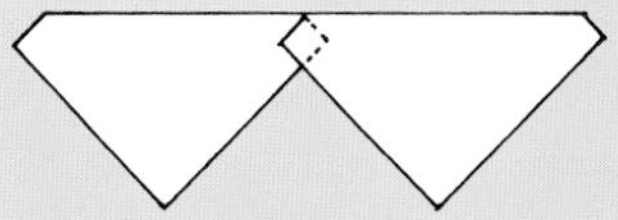

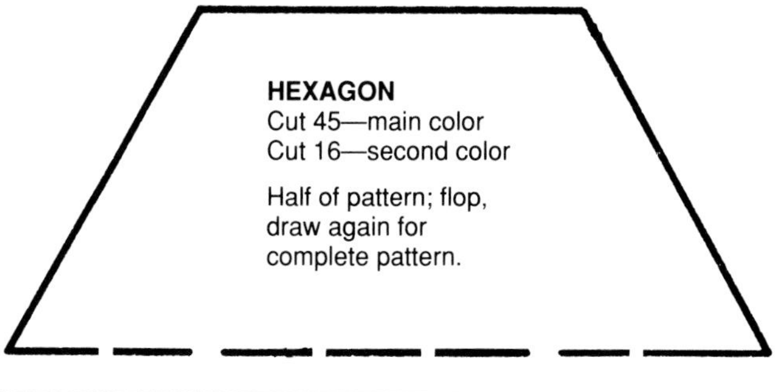

HEXAGON
Cut 45—main color
Cut 16—second color

Half of pattern; flop, draw again for complete pattern.

FATHER CHRISTMAS FOLK ART

THE country colors in this old-fashioned Santa banner will warm any room in your home! It would also make a great gift for a Santa collector.

APPLIQUE SANTA BANNER

Materials needed: Patterns; 1/2 yard each dark green and dark red cotton print fabric; 1/4 yard dark green cotton pindot fabric; 1/3 yard khaki cotton fabric; 1/4 yard featherweight iron-on interfacing; 1/2 yard lightweight batting; scraps of white, flesh and dark brown cotton fabric; scrap of light gray pindot fabric; 1/2 yard cotton muslin; water-soluble marker; fabric glue stick; two 1-inch bone or plastic rings; large bias tape maker; matching threads; standard sewing supplies.

Finished size: Banner measures about 17 inches square.

Directions: Prepare applique pieces first. Place interfacing, fusible side up, on pattern. Using water-soluble marker, trace four corner hearts and all Santa pieces individually. Cut

out all pieces roughly 1/4 inch from traced lines. With fusible side down, iron interfacing to wrong side of appropriate fabrics. Cut out each piece on traced lines.

Sandwich together khaki fabric, batting and muslin. Measure and cut a 12-1/2-inch square. Pin layers together along edges to prevent shifting. Using embroidery or applique foot on your machine and a scrap of layered fabric, test and establish stitch width, density and tension.

Position Santa pieces on layered square and tack them down with dabs of fabric glue. Using a medium-width satin zigzag stitch and matching threads, sew around pieces in order indicated on pattern. Using a wide-width satin zigzag stitch and making sure not to stitch over Santa's hand, sew staff from top to bottom, turn around and stitch from bottom to top.

Sandwich together dark green pindot fabric, batting and muslin. Measure and cut four 3-1/2-inch squares. Pin layers together along edges to prevent shifting. Zigzag hearts to layered squares using same method as before.

To make checkerboard border, cut four 16- x 2-inch strips from dark green pindot fabric and four 16- x 2-inch strips from khaki fabric. All following sewing steps use 1/4-inch seam allowances. Alternating colors, sew strips together along 16-inch edge. Press seams open. Placed striped piece right side down, stripes running horizontal. Measure and cut fabric into eight 2-inch-wide vertical strips. See Fig. 1.

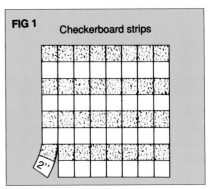

FIG 1 Checkerboard strips

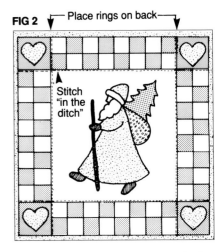

FIG 2 Place rings on back

Stitch "in the ditch"

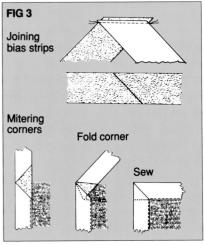

FIG 3

Joining bias strips

Mitering corners

Fold corner

Sew

With right sides together and alternating blocks, sew two strips together along one 16-inch edge. Repeat and sew three more pieces. Press seams open.

Cut four 3-1/2- x 12-1/2-inch batting strips. Layer and secure batting strips to checkerboard pieces with tiny dabs of glue. With right sides together, sew a checkerboard piece to right and left sides of appliqued Santa square. With right sides together, sew a heart square to each end of remaining checkerboard pieces and stitch

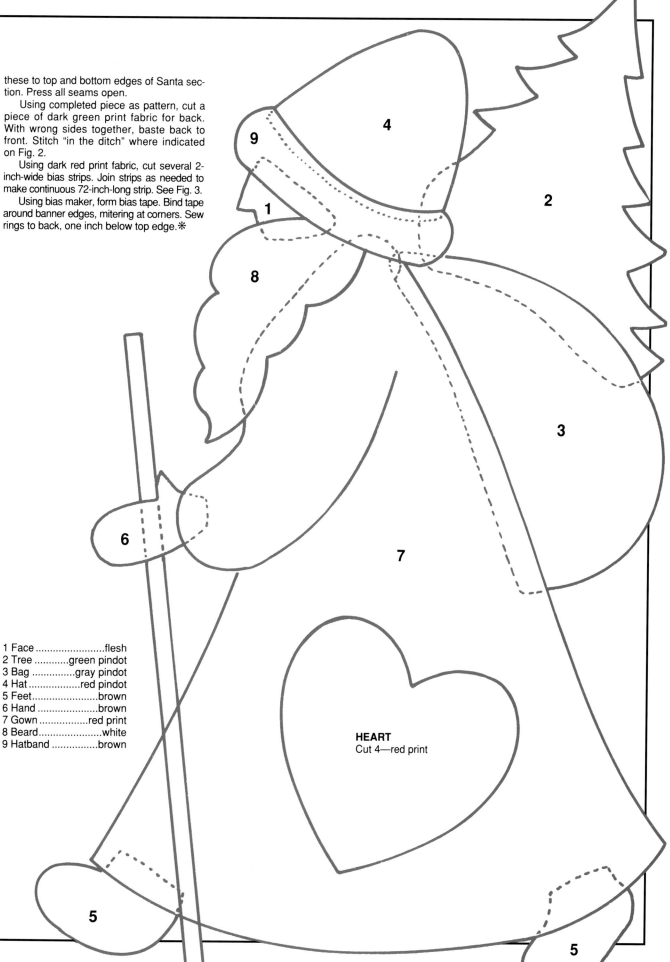

these to top and bottom edges of Santa section. Press all seams open.

Using completed piece as pattern, cut a piece of dark green print fabric for back. With wrong sides together, baste back to front. Stitch "in the ditch" where indicated on Fig. 2.

Using dark red print fabric, cut several 2-inch-wide bias strips. Join strips as needed to make continuous 72-inch-long strip. See Fig. 3.

Using bias maker, form bias tape. Bind tape around banner edges, mitering at corners. Sew rings to back, one inch below top edge.✽

4

9

2

1

8

3

6

7

1 Face ....flesh
2 Tree ....green pindot
3 Bag ....gray pindot
4 Hat ....red pindot
5 Feet.......................brown
6 Hand ....brown
7 Gown ....red print
8 Beard.....................white
9 Hatband ....brown

HEART
Cut 4—red print

5

5

She Wraps Kitchen for Christmas!

WHEN she decks her halls for the holidays, Carol Stephens of Waukesha, Wisconsin fills every corner with cheer. But her decorative doings aren't wrapped up until she gift-wraps her country kitchen—literally.

"I'm crazy about Christmas," Carol confides with a chuckle. "I've always decorated every room in the house. The kitchen and eating area never looked as pretty as I wanted, though…until I decided to cover the walls temporarily with Christmas wrapping paper!

"My husband, Edward, groaned when I got out the stepladder and a staple gun that Christmas a few years ago," Carol remembers. "I attached the wrapping paper up high near the ceiling, using lightweight staples…

and the tiny holes in my 'regular' wallpaper didn't show up *too* much after the holidays!"

Every Christmas since, Carol has hung bright wrapping paper right over her everyday wallpaper, "tying up" her wrapped room afterward with wide velvet ribbon borders along the ceiling.

Wrapping her kitchen completes days of decorating for Carol, who starts in the cozy family room with a row of beautiful burlap stockings on the mantel. Hooked by a family friend, there's one for each of the seven Stephens children.

A traditional tree trimmed in red and green stands nearby. But *one* tree indoors isn't enough for this dedicated decorator! A second tree towers

in the living room, trimmed with one-of-a-kind ornaments in hues of rose and blue to match the daily decor. A wooden sleigh sporting the same colors brims with boughs and gifts.

December dining's a delight at Carol's festive table, set with holiday dinnerware and graced with a simple centerpiece of pinecones and greenery. Carol drapes her chandelier in greens and clears her knickknack shelf to showcase her collection of Nativity sets.

All that delightful decorating takes time, but Carol doesn't mind. "I love every minute of it!" she confides.

And, she adds, she does get an *early* start. The day after Christmas, she shops post-holiday sales for the next year's kitchen wrap!

WRAPPED UP in happy holiday cheer, Carol Stephens creates festive feelings indoors and out with a tree trimmed on the patio and prettily "packaged" walls!

ALL THROUGH THE HOUSE. Feast for the eyes greets guests in dining room, left, while wooden sleigh stuffed with gifts helps Santa on his way. Below left, stockings, bow-bedecked bear and "Rudolph" warm hearth, while garlands of blue and rose pose a new look for the living room Christmas tree.

89

Decorative Windows & Doors

BEAUTIFUL BAY window (right) roped with greenery, red lights and lacquered apples adds appealing color to Lanore Thumma's dining room in Laurens, Iowa. Authentic Swedish straw wreaths and quilted valance (above) contribute country charm, too.

Here's a peek at some of the best-dressed doors and window decor in the country. Give guests a warm holiday welcome by following a few of these imaginative ideas!

WOODEN WREATH is carefully crafted of clothespins for kitchen window (below) at Linda Sharp's Shelocta, Pennsylvania home. Stenciled frame sets off pane, pine aligns sill, candles glow as apples sway from ribbons.

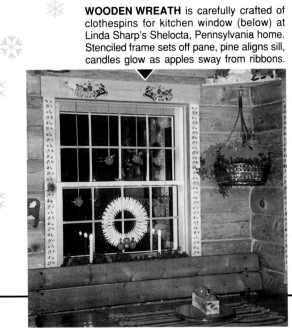

LACY FLAKES of snow add winter wonderment to the window treatment at Heidi Hoffman's country home in Mequon, Wisconsin. Bright balls, greenery grace ledge above; cuddly country critters cavort on the sill below.

BEST FOOT forward greets guests at Karen Gardiner's front door in Eutaw, Alabama. Created from an old quilt, stocking's stuffed with merry magnolia leaves, bright berries, baby's breath.

MAKING MERRY makes doing dishes delightful for Beverly Swanson in Red Oak, Iowa! Pine and blue spruce add to scenery above bay window, beside sink. Candles, lights, bows, snowflakes and grapevine wreath also brighten kitchen.

WHEAT WEARS WELL in Phyllis Boyd's decor in Lake Preston, South Dakota. Farm-grown grain with red bows graces, boughs, while snowflakes swirl in windowpanes.

TEA FOR TWO sets seasonal scene in Sandra Csippan's bay window in Lafayette, New Jersey. Sandra, who is big on bears, sewed clothes, designed hats, cut out cookies for furry friends.

BRIGHT, BEARDED Santa is "doorman" for family and friends stepping into Linda Clarke's kitchen in Havelock, New Brunswick. Century-old door (above) is also decked with moss, bows and gingerbread cookies.

She Crafts Christmas in Every Corner

By Nancy McNeil Cornell, Dallas, Texas

FROM driftwood to fence posts, country crafter Karen Lee's taking Kris Kringle to new heights. In fact, folks around Salado, Texas wouldn't be surprised if she *did* head for the rooftops soon!

Karen's antique shop, the Dusty Rose, has a Christmas presence year-round, thanks to the hundreds of handmade Santa shapes she stocks on the walls and shelves —all the product of her penchant for putting the jolly old elf anywhere she can.

"I'll paint Santas on planters, handsaws, fence pickets—even rolling pins," she grins—not to mention seashells, shovels, ironing boards and arrowheads!

Delivering Christmas cheer 365 days a year, she admits, seems at times like a dream to her. And, perhaps, that's due to the way Karen's unusual crafting interest commenced. "I woke up in the middle of the night a couple years ago," she recalls. "For some reason, I was thinking of old-fashioned Santas—even though it wasn't Christmastime.

"Then, the next morning, I found a piece of driftwood by the creek. It reminded me of Santa, too. I took it home…painted the knotholes into eyes…the root into a beard—and soon there were Santas everywhere I turned!"

To make her Santas stand out even further—"Every one is different," she affirms—Karen turned to her roots.

"When I started painting my Santas, I knew just what shade of red I wanted—the shade of the red barns I grew up with in Iowa. And that's exactly what they are!"

But then, Karen can transform the simplest bits of country into Christmas collectibles. "The old cedar stumps in the pastures near my home naturally have the essence of Santa," she's discovered. "And the gourds I buy from local farmers are another perfect surface.

"To make sure they keep their antique appearance, I finish all my Santas with a country pine stain," Karen confides. Sometimes, she'll even rub sandpaper over their dimples, since her customers seem to prefer their Santas with a well-seasoned charm.

While keeping in the Christmas spirit, Karen's branched out into a new line of holiday handcrafts. "My ornaments are becoming popular, too, as tree decorations and Christmas cards," she informs. "I cut them from thin plywood into all sorts of shapes—crescent moons and cowboy boots, for example.

"Around here, though," she adds with a Lone Star State laugh, "my top seller is an ornament in the shape of the state of Texas!"

Even during a dusty Southwest summer afternoon, though, Santa never strays far from her thoughts. "A wood carver I met loaned me his knife and gave me some lessons on whittling," she smiles. "Now, I can really make some interesting Santas!"

And with a flick of her brush, Karen adds the finishing touch to the face of yet another…well, you know who-ho-ho!

For more on Karen's Santas, you can write her at P.O. Box 793, Salado TX 76571.

NONSTOP SHOP. Karen Lee whittles, paints and decks the walls of her craft store with Santas all year.

JOY TO THE WORLD

Isaac Watts

George F. Handel

1. Joy to the world! the Lord is come; Let earth re-
2. Joy to the earth! the Sav-ior reigns; Let men their
3. No more let sins and sor-rows grow, Nor thorns in-the
4. He rules the world with truth and grace, And makes the

ceive her King; Let ev-'ry heart pre-pare Him room,
songs em-ploy; While fields and floods, rocks, hills and plains
fest the ground; He comes to make His bless-ings flow
na-tions prove The glo-ries of His right-eous-ness,

And heav'n and na-ture sing, And heav'n and na-ture
Re-peat the sound-ing joy, Re-peat the sound-ing
Far as the curse is found, Far as the curse is
And won-ders of His love, And won-ders of His
(1.)And heav'n and na-ture sing, And

sing, And heav'n and heav'n and na-ture sing.
joy, Re-peat, re-peat the sound-ing joy.
found, Far as, far as the curse is found.
love, And won-ders, and won-ders of His love.
heav'n and na-ture sing,

Their Christmas Carol

When their barn burned down, this Pennsylvania dairy family thought they were finished...but as it turned out, it was the beginning of a whole new life.

By Roy Reiman

THIS STORY actually started during one of our fall tours to Switzerland, when my wife and I were escorting a group of 80-some couples.

As is customary on each of our World Wide Country Tours, we had each couple stand up and introduce themselves, telling who they were, where they were from and a little about their area. Once that's done, we find we can travel as one big friendly "family".

Anyway, as introductions were going along, one nice-looking farm couple stood up, and the man said, "We're Paul and Pat Miller...the famous 'Singing Millers' from Harrisburg, Pennsylvania." Then, with a subtle smile, he added, "If you haven't heard of us, it gives you an idea of just how famous we are..."

When he finished talking about their farm, I asked him—since they were the "Famous Singing Millers" —whether he and his wife would sing for our group. Sure, he replied, and with no rehearsal, he and Pat strode up to the little stage area and sang three verses of *Edelweiss* that absolutely brought down the house.

Their harmony was fantastic, and they sang with such feeling many of our tour members got tears in their eyes. (Me, too—I'm a real softie.) They sounded like professionals, and got a deserved standing ovation when they finished.

They *Were* Famous

Later during the tour, my wife and I got Paul and Pat aside and asked just how a dairy couple like them had become such talented singers. The story they told really moved us...

"It all began in 1970," Paul related. "Our three kids were just getting old enough to help, our herd was growing in size and production, and things were going smoothly.

"Then the roof fell in. In late July, I was seriously injured in an auto accident and was laid up in the hospital for most of a month—just as harvest was beginning. Well, if it hadn't been for our neighbors, our farm operation wouldn't have survived—they all helped Pat and the kids with our cows and put up all of our crops.

"Of course, none of them would take a penny. I had plenty of time to think about that, lying in that hospital bed, and I concluded that God has a reason for everything, including sparing my life."

Tragedy Strikes Again

Paul and Pat had to endure another test of that faith just 2 months later when, shortly after their neighbors had completed storing their crops for the winter, the Millers' dairy barn—and all those stored crops—burned to the ground.

"Those same neighbors came to our aid once more," Paul recalled, his voice tight with emotion. "They took our cows—a few here, a few there—and milked them with their herds. To put it bluntly, Pat and I were terribly depressed and discouraged.

"I figured we'd had it—there was no way we could get a new barn up before the winter closed in. But our neighbors wouldn't have it. Our pastor announced a 'cleanup day' at our place, and more than 80 people showed up!

"They not only cleaned up the mess, but they ordered the lumber,

"I concluded God has a reason for everything, including sparing my life."

got a local contractor to help, and in 2 days they had the framework of a new barn standing. They kept coming back, and we had our herd back in our own barn before the first snow fell.

"As Christmas approached that year, we had a lot to be thankful for," Paul said, "and we just *had* to come up with some way of showing our appreciation to our fantastic neighbors. I thought about it a lot as I worked, and finally I said to Pat, 'Would those people think it was corny if we went to each of their farms and sang Christmas carols?'

"Now, I should point out that I've always loved to sing. It's sort of my hobby. Some people fish or hunt or play golf...I've always sung for enjoyment. It's a hobby I can enjoy even when I'm working. Pat loves to sing, too, and I guess it brushed off on the kids.

"Well, we couldn't come up with anything better, so we practiced a few songs and went out Christmas caroling after we got done milking each night. We couldn't believe the reception we got—people told us it was the nicest thing we could have done, and that we had added a lot more meaning to their Christmas.

"We went out night after night—

Lasted More Than 8 Years

we could only stop at five or six farms a night. I recall we were rather hesitant to go to this one farm, because those people were sort of quiet and, well, regarded as a little 'different'. But they'd helped us, so we decided to risk it. Well, when we finished singing for them, they came right out and hugged us. It really choked us up."

Became Well-Known

The neighbors who heard the Miller family were not only impressed by the gesture, but by their obvious singing *talent*. Word spread, and soon requests began pouring in for appearances by "The Singing Millers" at churches and gatherings across Pennsylvania.

It wasn't easy to work all day, milk in the evening, and then sing in a program 100 miles away one night, and 100 miles the other direction the next night. "But we just couldn't turn anyone down," Paul said. "The rewards were so great—seeing the pleasure on people's faces as they heard our family sing, and hearing their words of praise and encouragement meant so much to us."

A few stories appeared in Pennsylvania papers and beyond, one thing led to another, and soon "The Singing Millers" were on their road to fame, beginning what turned out to be an 8-year sideline of semi-professional singing.

They recorded a commercial used nationally by the Babson Bros. dairy supply firm…cut their first record in 1973 (*He's Got the Whole World in His Hands*, dedicated to all the people who had helped them in 1970)… cut another record, *Music to Believe In*…and were selected as the featured entertainment at the 1976 National Holstein Convention in Philadelphia.

"That was probably our biggest thrill," Pat said of the convention appearance. "That was the Bicentennial year, so we added some patriotic songs to our medley and had a fan blowing on the American flag behind us. We got a standing ovation after the show, and we'll never forget that.

"The incredible part of all this was that Paul and the boys still managed to milk and breed a herd of cows and kept them in top production and test."

Another thrill came when daughter Deb was crowned Pennsylvania Dairy Princess. She was the first "singing princess", and sang many times on radio and TV—with her family singing "backup".

Wedding Bells Broke 'Em Up

The kids grew older, and late in 1978, wedding bells and college started breaking up the Miller gang. It became more difficult to get together as they sang through the winter of 1978, so they recorded a final album, *To God Be the Glory*, and made their last public appearance as a group on January 1, 1979.

"I guess you could say we're back to being a 'normal' dairy family now," Pat said with a grin, "except that our cows all have musical names!

"Music is still a very important part of our lives…especially at Christmastime, when we get the kids and all of their families together for some caroling."

"We'll never forget that Christmas in 1970, though," Paul said. "We thought God was being pretty hard on us…but He just had a much bigger plan for us. Our songs of thanks reached a lot more people than we ever thought possible when we first began to 'repay' our neighbors with a few amateur Christmas carols."

AMATEURS. This is how the Miller family looked when they began singing in 1970.

Miracle of Christmas Comes Home

By Nancy Painter
Treherne, Manitoba

THE Christmas season is just as hectic at our house as yours, I'm sure! It takes a conscious effort to make time to tell the story of our little wooden creche...to emphasize the giving instead of the receiving...and to spend time together as a family.

But when we find ourselves losing sight of the holiday's real meaning, we can always recall an event that lovingly reminds us of what's truly important this time of year.

Our daughter, Amy, was born on December 22. Oh, the joy of that first child! Our very own Christmas miracle, with perfect little fingers and toes and even a complexion that looked days old.

But little Amy wasn't quite perfect, we soon discovered. The other mothers were allowed to keep their babies in their rooms while ours was confined to the nursery. Her birth had been difficult—and there was growing concern about the ominous swelling inside her head.

I ached to nurse my firstborn. But the closest I could come was to help a nurse feed her through the tube in her mouth. Scrubbed up and in a surgical gown, I felt heartbreakingly distant.

Christmas Day brought a brief, subdued celebration back at our farm...and then a frightening development in the dark of the next morning. Our little Amy's heart was literally stopping, and she was being rushed to a larger hospital and the hands of experts.

My husband held me as a deacon from our church hurried to baptize our precious daughter before the ambulance sped her away. The solemn words and motions as he reached around the tubes to touch her head cut through our fear to give us comfort.

That comfort continued as we encountered one caring person after another—the nurses in the new intensive care nursery, who told us honestly what they did and didn't know...the doctor, an important man in a large hospital, who phoned us from his home on his Sunday off to answer our questions and allay our fears.

But it was the smallest of gestures that meant the most. When a Christmas stocking of small gifts

❦

"Oh, the joy of that first child!"

appeared on Amy's incubator, I seized its presence as a symbol. Every child in the hospital received such a stocking, but to me, Amy's confirmed that someone besides us had faith.

I *knew* then that Amy would survive to play with those toys.

And that faith proved right.

The swelling in her head slowly subsided, and Amy left her incubator behind. Finally, I could bathe and, best of all, feed her.

She came home to the farm just as the New Year began. How fitting that timing seemed!

Since that happy homecoming, Amy has grown from a frail infant into an energetic and loving 4-year-old. But each December, when the demands of the season weigh most heavily, we step back and marvel anew over our own Christmas miracle. As we do, we think of another, even greater miracle.

There was, after all, a Christmas Child born long ago in strange and hostile circumstances who has changed the lives of all who have known Him.

And when we think of Amy... when we think of Him...we know again where the joy of Christmas is to be found.